Christianity versus violence

Christianity versus Violence

A social and historical study of
war and christianity

Stanley Windass

Sheed and Ward
London

CONTENTS
PART 1

CONTENTS

PART 2

CONTENTS

PART 3

PART 1

1. THE PROTEST

"Those whom the Christian has put to flight in the daytime by exorcisms, shall he defend them by night, leaning and resting on the lance with which Christ's side was pierced? And shall he carry a flag too that is rival to Christ's?"[1]
TERTULLIAN

THE early Christians certainly thought of themselves as a fighting force, resembling in many ways the army of the Roman Emperor. Their concern, however, was not with material but with spiritual enemies; not with the enemies of Rome, but with the enemies of Christ, who were none other than the devil and his "legions", the forces of evil engaged in perpetual warfare against mankind and the kingdom of God which Christ had founded.

From the beginning, the life of Jesus had been depicted by the Evangelists as a contest with Satan. The story began with the Temptation in the Wilderness; it was continued by the frequent exorcisms and miracles of healing, which showed that the power of the devil was broken; and it was consummated on Calvary, by way of suffering and obedience to death. It was at these points in the Gospels that the invisible spiritual battle emerged to the surface.

The story, however, did not end on Calvary. The Disciples were commissioned to carry out an extensive mopping-up operation. Together with the power to preach, they were given the power to cast out spirits, and so to show the authority of their victorious king

It is quite obvious from all the early accounts that exorcisms were an important part of the Apostles' activities, and an important proof of their claims; for it was always in the name of Christ that they did their casting out—and nobody, not even the most capable of their opponents, seems to be able to deny that they *could* cast out devils! "Even the demonic powers", wrote Tertullian, "are forced to bear witness to us"[2]; and, whatever he meant, it was obviously true.

The devils were public personalities as well as private individuals. They were not only considered to be the source of all kinds of diseases, mental, moral, and physical; they were also identified with the pagan gods, the images of wood and stone which the Christians took such a delight in overthrowing, and considered to be the source of public as well as private calamities. In a sense, what seems to us the "superstition" of the early Church was nothing else than their fight against superstition—if they said that there was a devil in a piece of wood, it was to deny that there was a god in it, and therefore to deny that it had any effective power. The whole world and the atmosphere around it was imagined to be filled with spirits, sitting on thrones, hovering around cradles, and influencing every phase of life—but all were creatures of the one true God, and either ministering to him, or powerless against him, and equally powerless against the faith of Christians. The demonology and exorcisms of the early Christians may have been a way of bringing to a head the disorders of a society living among the decaying ruins of ancient religions; and, by bringing them to a head, bringing them nearer to a cure, just as morbid matter can be discharged from the body once it has been gathered into a cyst.

Since the Church was involved in this battle, it had to be organized and armed like a military force; but its weapons were the weapons of the spirit, the only ones that are any use against enemies who *are* spirits. St Paul had first described the equipment of the Christian soldier[3]—the breastplate of faith and love, the helmet of hope, and the sword of the spirit, and later this language become more and more popular as a whole pattern of military thinking was borrowed into Christianity. Christians were *militia Christi*, the soldiers of Christ; the Church was their camp, and Christ their emperor; heretics and schismatics are rebels and traitors. Even the word "sacrament", which later became a key word in theology, was borrowed from the Roman army; the *sacramentum* was the military oath, by which the Roman soldier bound himself to the "divine" Emperor, and was adopted by the Christians to describe the baptism by which they dedicated themselves to the service of the *real* God.

Evidently there is some positive inspiration here—the dedication of the Roman soldier inspires the Christian to even greater dedication, and often the discipline and organization of the Roman army are admired, from a distance, by early Christian writers. The important thing to remember, however, is that however much the Christians borrowed military language, they were always *opposing* their type of warfare to the warfare of the legions. Material war was one thing, but spiritual war was another—and much more serious. Indeed, the material warfare of the Roman armies is very much like the work of the devil himself. It is, as Tertullian says, "the camp of darkness", and there is nothing in common between the camp of light and the camp of darkness. The mirror-image of Roman militarism which we find in early Christian records is also a reversal of it, a reaction-formation within the body politic of the Roman State.

Stirring up wars was in fact thought to be one of the favourite hobbies of the devil himself and his agents. We read in Justinus how "nations, intoxicated by the devil, sharpen up their passions for murderous battles"; and the great historian of the early Church, Eusebius, tries to prove that nations have become more and more peaceful as the demons which used to goad them into war have been progressively subdued by the Christians, along with the polytheistic error which kept them from the true faith. The demons and the false gods were, of course, the same; and it was easy to see them as the provokers of all human strife, since the gods had always played a prominent part in war.

It is impossible to appreciate the attitude of the early Church to war unless we can recapture something of its vision; and, since it is a vision which can only be recaptured in poetry, it is to the actual words of the early Fathers that we should go. Nothing recaptures the vision more splendidly than a little poem of Clement of Alexandria, written in the second century:

Now the trumpet sounds with a mighty voice, calling
    the soldiers of the world to arms, announcing war;

And shall not Christ, who has uttered his summons
    to peace even to the ends of the earth,
Summon together his own soldiers of peace?
Indeed, O Man, he has called to arms with his blood
    and his word an army that sheds no blood;
To these soldiers he has handed over the Kingdom
    of Heaven.
The trumpet of Christ is his gospel. He has sounded
    it in our ears and we have heard it.
Let us be armed for peace, putting on the armour
    of justice, seizing the shield of faith,
The helmet of salvation,
And sharpening the sword of the spirit which is the
    word of God.
This is how the Apostle prepares us peacefully for
    battle.
Such are the arms that make us invulnerable.
So armed, let us prepare to fight the Evil One.
Let us cut through his flaming attack with the blade
    which the Logos himself has tempered in the
    waters of baptism.
Let us reply to his goodness by praise and thanks-
    giving.
Let us honour God with his divine word:
"While thou art yet speaking," he says, "here I am."[4]

1. No Bloodshed

Within this pattern of the spiritual war, powerful
moral concepts were organized which had a lasting
influence on the conscience of Christendom. Not the
least of these moral forces was the abhorrence of blood-

shed, and the attack on the sins of hatred and anger, from which all human strife was seen to proceed.

Already in the Jewish tradition the shedding of blood, or indeed any contact with blood whether of men or of animals, was regarded with something like superstitious horror. To this day, the Jews will not taste the blood of animals; and the rather puzzling ceremony, still retained in the Christian Church, of the "purification" of women after childbirth seems to point to the same revulsion. In the story of the Crucifixion, at the point of transition between Judaism and Christianity, it is recorded that the chief priests would not receive the thirty pieces of silver from Judas into the treasury of the Temple, because they were the price of "blood".[5]

The Christians, whose traditions are of course continuous with those of the Jews, inherited these ideas, but gave them an even more central importance and a deeper spiritual significance. The earliest Church rules still forbid the receipt of money from magistrates polluted by war,[6] and abstention from the blood even of animals remained the general rule; but it became even more clear for the Christians than for the Jews that the murder of Abel by Cain was indeed the "archetypal" crime, the pattern of all human strife and bloodshed. The sin of murder was regarded with the utmost horror, and murderers were permanently excluded from the Christian community. An important writer in the time of the Emperor Constantine expressed most clearly the spiritual insight behind this revulsion from blood when he wrote, "Man is so sacrosanct a creature that it is always wrong to kill him . . .

no exception can be made to this commandment of God."[7]

Anger and hatred are always condemned along with bloodshed; the ideas seem to be inseparable. No-one can be considered just who "injures, hates, despoils and kills".[8] St John had written that "every man who hates his brother is a murderer",[9] and the early Fathers held fast to this insight.

No distinction was made between public and private behaviour; the fact that something was done on the authority of the State did not alter its moral quality. Public executions were morally the same, for a Christian, as any other killing; people who witnessed and took pleasure in a public execution were in the same condition as witnesses to a private murder.[10] It is often pointed out that men abhor killing on a small scale, and yet glory in it on a large scale, as in war.[11] A Christian could not possibly administer judicial punishments, for how could they, who would not even avenge their own wrongs, "administer chains, and imprisonments, and executions, in order to avenge the wrongs of another"?[12]

This was only the negative side of a very positive teaching deriving from the Sermon on the Mount. The early Christians considered themselves under an obligation to love their enemies, to respond to curses with prayers, to violence with gentleness; for, in so doing, they exercised a *greater power* than that of their enemies, the power of the triumphant Christ, who had conquered the forces of evil in this way on Calvary. The hero-ideal was always the martyr—and it was (and is) an essential condition of martyrdom that suffering should be freely accepted, and not violently resisted. That this ideal was very commonly realized by ordinary folk is one of the astonishing facts of the first age of Christianity; people were sometimes so eager for martyrdom that the difficulty was rather to hold them back from offering themselves rashly to the executioners' torments.

2. No Military Service

Not unnaturally, these Christians did not regard service in the Roman legions as a very suitable occupation.

Until somewhere near the end of the second century, the question of military service did not arise in an acute form for the Christian community. There is no authentic evidence for the existence of a single Christian soldier after that of the New Testament, until about A.D. 170; but, at the same time, there is no clear regulation prohibiting military service for Christians. Neither of these negative bits of information is very significant on its own, although they have been much over-worked in the pacifist-anti-pacifist debate of recent times. The fact is that the Romans never had universal conscription, and no-one was actually bound to serve in the army, save in exceptional circumstances. As there was not the slightest pressure on Christians to serve, and as the opposition between the spirit of Christ and the spirit of the Roman legions was self-evident, there was really no need to argue about it or to make rules about it and unnecessarily antagonize imperial authority.

Towards the end of the second century, however, two things start to happen which are closely connected. Evidence begins to appear of an increasing number of Christians serving in the army; and, at the same time, theologians begin to say quite clearly that they must not do so. Evidently, the question has become a real one. The tide of conversion is rising, and there are many converts in the army, as elsewhere; should they all desert, or should they not? Christianity is becoming more an accepted part of society, and a man can be an ambitious and patriotic Roman as well as a Christian; must he then renounce his military ambitions? As the opposition of the Church to the world becomes blurred, so the question of military service becomes acute.

The first answers of the theologians, however, were not at all blurred. Against the rising pressures they took a clear stand. The Christian was to wage a spiritual war, not a carnal one; and he must use the sword against no-one. Sometimes, in the course of their arguments, we catch a glimpse of the arguments on the other side, the arguments of those who were trying to find some way of reconciling Christianity with military service. "Moses carried a rod . . . Aaron wore a buckle . . . the Israelites fought . . ."[13] Simple, literal arguments from the Old Testament, which were by no means hard to refute. It is not surprising that these militarist arguments are recorded for us only by chance, in the course of the counter-arguments of the pacifists, and do not otherwise survive. They are not the arguments of scholars, or of religious leaders—but rather of ordinary folk trying to accommodate their consciences to an uncomfortable situation.

The words of Christ to Peter in the Garden of Gethsemane, "He who takes the sword shall perish by the sword", were much quoted, because they came the closest to an actual ruling. Origen, commenting on this text at the end of the second century, tells us that Christ wanted us to put away the warlike sword and to take the sword of the spirit; and that we must beware lest "for warfare, or *for the vindication of our rights, or for any occasion*, we should take out the sword, for no such occasion is allowed by this evangelical teaching".[14]

These opinions are quite clear-cut, and there is no evidence at all that they represent only one stream of thought—still less that they are eccentric to the main tradition of the Church, as some scholars have tried to prove. All the evidence suggests, on the contrary, that this was the *only* stream of *thought*—though not the only stream of practice! Opinions, however, are still not regulations; the nearest we can get to official regulations about military service in this period are the *Canons of St Hippolytus*.[15]

Hippolytus was a Roman churchman, who drew up a list of rules for all matters of Church discipline, some time in the first part of the third century. His "canons", as they came to be called, are a mine of information for the traditions of the period at which he writes, and he is, on the whole, very conservative and very accurate. The main purpose of his work, as he says himself, is to "defend the traditional practices of the Church against the recent error and apostasy of ignorant men". Two of his canons concerned the question of military service; and, in spite of the obscurity of later versions, there is very little doubt about what these two canons originally conveyed. One said that a man could not be received as a Christian if he was in the army of the Emperor; and the other said that a catechumen who showed military ambitions was to be rejected, because "[this] is far from the Lord".[16]

The canons are the nearest we can get to the "law of the Church" for this period, and, as they were very popular, we can reasonably conclude that the army was just "against the law" at this time for a large number of Christians—in spite of the fact that there were lots of them in the army! This does not mean, however, that it was just a theoretical rule; from the end of the third century we have evidence of a much more live kind for the persistence of the pacifist ideal. A young African called Maximilian was summoned before the Proconsul to serve in the army (he was the son of a veteran, and was therefore one of the few who had an obligation to serve); but he refused simply on the grounds that he was a Christian and "could not do evil". He stuck to his point in spite of the persuasiveness of the Proconsul, who observed that there were many Christians in the Army; and as a result he was led away to execution.[17] This gave Christians a pacifist martyr, and he did not have to wait long for popular canonization. Though his fame has understandably waned since, his story has importance for the reality of the moral protest against military service even after three centuries of coexistence with the Roman State.

3. No Participation in Public Affairs

Military service was rejected because of its bloody nature; but it was also rejected because, for the higher ranks, army service meant taking a sacrilegious oath to a so-called "divine" emperor, and taking part in other idolatrous practices. From this point of view, moreover, it was just as bad to be a magistrate as to be a soldier; and if we have no evidence for the existence of Christian soldiers before the end of the second century, we have no evidence that Christians held any position of responsibility or authority under the Roman State until the middle of the third century. There is no doubt either, that this was a matter of principle. It was considered virtually impossible to reconcile the Christian conscience with "service to the pagan State", which seemed inevitably to involve sacrifices, oath-taking, tortures, imprisonments, and all manner of diabolical pomp.

Nor did Christians appear much in the pagan courts. They would never sue for their rights; and in the earliest summary of Church discipline, the *Didaskalia*, it is expressly forbidden for them to do so. Occasionally they appeared as defendants; but never as plaintiffs or, of course, as lawyers.

The reasons why the Christians kept away from the courts and from politics were not quite the same as the reasons why they kept away from the army; but all the same, this did all seem to add up to a general pattern of withdrawal, of "keeping away" from public life and responsibility, of general protest against the established order. Some of the livelier spirits expressed open antagonism against the Roman Empire, identifying it, as Hippolytus did, with the various beasts of the prophetic books. More generally, an attempt was made to appease the monster, to render unto Caesar what was Caesar's, and to recall that it derived its authority from God. All the same, there was a factual element about Christian withdrawal from public life which was undeniable.

Christians thought of themselves as a new people, a new community in Christ, which cut across national boundaries and dissolved local patriotisms. This meant, to some extent, that they had a *rival* organization, the embryo of a new order which would replace the old. When Origen has to defend his fellow Christians against the charge of evading public responsibility, he argues that they belong to another organization, and that those who are capable of leadership, far from evading responsibility, are reserving themselves for "a different and more necessary service".[18]

If Christians regarded themselves as a race apart it is not surprising that their non-Christian fellows regarded them in the same light, though with much less favour. They were often considered to be a foreign and disruptive element in the body politic; as a people who "shun the light of day, silent in public but garrulous in corners"; despising the sacred things of the State, recognizing each other by secret signs and tokens, and "loving each other almost before they are acquainted". This is a typical group protest against a foreign and dangerous element; it is not surprising that the Christians were told sometimes to "get out of the world where they did not belong". They acquired the common title of the "Third Race". The first race was the ordinary people, the second race the Jews, who "stood apart", and the third race was the Christians who were even stranger than the Jews. In view of this, they were often made the scapegoat for public calamities; indeed their "apartheid" does much to explain the early persecutions, just as it later explained the persecutions of the Jews.

4. THE CHARGE OF DISLOYALTY

The most systematic effort to defend Christians against the charge of disloyalty was made by Origen; and it is worth following his argument carefully, because it takes us right into the mind of the early Church, and in some ways foreshadows things to come.

The defence is found in a book called *Contra Celsum*,[19] which is a reply to a pagan philosopher who had made an elaborate attack on Christianity. In particular, he had argued that "if all did as the Christians do"—that is, if no-one entered the service of the State —"the Emperor would be left alone and deserted, and earthly things would fall into the hands of lawless and savage barbarians"; moreover, he had said, it would then be all over with the Christians' precious worship and wisdom—they would have cut off the branch on which they were sitting.

Origen argues shrewdly. First, he asks, where would the savage barbarians come from, if "all did as the Christians did"? Celsus, of course, had not really meant all—he had only meant all the *real people*—that is, all the Romans! Origen's point, however, is well made;

for a Christian, everyone must mean "everyone"—and Christ is among the barbarians as well. The fraternal love of Christians can know no boundaries; and Origen seems to visualize a gradual extension of the Word like a great sea of peace over the whole surface of the earth, until all cause of violence is removed, and the symptom of war disappears.

Having made his point, Origen, in all fairness, deals with what Celsus really *meant*; what if all the *Romans* were converted and the barbarians were not? Would Rome then not be defenceless against invasion? There are only two ways out of this: one is to appeal to the ideal of martyrdom, and the other is to rely on super- natural intervention. Not even Origen can suggest "group martyrdom" as a sensible ideal for Rome; so he takes the second line. If all Romans were Christian and refused to fight, Rome would nevertheless not fall, and Rome would not be sacked; Christ has promised that if even two of us agree to pray for something it will be given to us—and what could not the whole of Rome do if it were united in prayer? Just as the Israelites were protected against the Egyptians who were destroyed in the Red Sea, so the Romans would certainly be preserved by the same divine power. In this way the purity of the Christian ideal is preserved, and the political difficulty is resolved; but only by bringing the supernatural directly into the political arena—by a sort of *deus-ex-machina* argument, which avoids completely the difficulty of the natural organiza- tion of society.

Origen still has the more urgent problems to con- sider; quite apart from what might happen if all

Romans were Christians, what about the present situation, in which the Christian minority profits from the
protection of the Roman State but does not contribute
to it? Are they not a kind of spiritual Fifth Column?
To this challenge, Origen's answer is partly natural
and partly supernatural. Christians, he says, give an
alternative service of a different nature to that of the
soldier, but in harmony with it. They work continuously
for the improvement of the moral fibre of the citizen,
which is of benefit to the whole State; and they provide a powerhouse of prayer. They pray in particular
for the suppression of the demons who stir up wars,
violate oaths, and disturb the peace—and they also
pray for those who "fight in a righteous cause". This
alternative service, he claims, should be allowed, in
the same way that the pagan priests are allowed to
keep their hands undefiled by blood for the sake of
offering sacrifice.

"Christians pray for those who fight in a righteous
cause"—the phrase has been eagerly pounced on by
all those who have tried to find in the early Fathers
the basis for the elaborate justification of war which
emerged centuries later. Scholarship of this kind is
mistaken. It is clear that when Origen talks about
Christians praying for those who fight in a just war,
he is not for a moment suggesting that Christians could
themselves fight in such a war—nor is he necessarily
saying that Christians are endorsing the fighting by
their prayers—for you can pray for a soldier without
necessarily praying for a bloody victory, and indeed
without praying for military victory at all. All the same,
there is certainly a recognition that there can be *in*

some sense "a just cause", and this may well be regarded as the beginning of a long history of concessions which Christianity was obliged to make to a society of which it was forming an increasingly important part.

NOTES

[1] Tertullian, *De Corona Militis* (*PL* 2, 92).

[2] Tertullian, *Apologia*, ch. 46; discussed by Harnack, *Expansion of Christianity*, trans. Moffat, New York (1904), pp. 152–80.

[3] 1 Thess. 5.8–9; Eph. 6.17.

[4] Quoted by Thomas Merton in *Clement of Alexandria*, *Selections from the Protreptikos*, New Directions (1962).

[5] Matt. 27.6.

[6] *Didaskalia IV*, 4, quoted by Cadoux, *Early Christian Attitude to War*, p. 53.

[7] Lactantius, *Institutes*, 6, 22, 17.

[8] Lactantius, 6, 6, 22.

[9] 1 John 3.15.

[10] Lactantius, 6, 20, 10; quoted by Cadoux, p. 159.

[11] Lactantius, 1, 18, 8–10; quoted by Cadoux, p. 56.

[12] *PL*, 2, 92.

[13] *PL*, 1, 690–91.

[14] Origen, *Works*, Berlin Corpus ed., vol. 11, pp. 221–2.

[15] Ed. Gregory Dix in *The Apostolic Tradition*, London, S.P.C.K. (1937). The various texts of the relevant canons are quoted in full in Cadoux, pp. 122–3.

[16] From the Ethiopean version of the canons; see preceding note.

[17] Ruinart, *Acta Martyrum*, Ratisbon (1859), pp. 341–2.

[18] Origen, *Contra Celsum*, 8, 74; quoted by Cadoux, p. 136.

[19] Origen, *Contra Celsum*, ed. and trans. Chadwick, pp. 504–10.

2. THE ACCOMMODATION

1. INCREASING TENSIONS

CELSUS' complaint about the early Christian attitudes to the State had not been without foundation. The Christian community of the first centuries had in fact been in an odd position; it had lived within the structure of Roman society without accepting responsibility for it—in a sense it had taken while refusing to give. The oddness was reflected in doctrine. From the beginning there had been a tendency to use two different standards of morality, one for "them", the people responsible for the government of society, and another, a higher one, for "us", that is, for the Christian group living within that society. Origen's mention of "those who fight in a just cause" in the very same book which is written to justify the Christian refusal to fight, is only one symptom of this kind of "double thinking".

The tradition of the special kind of "rightness" belonging to what the State does was built mainly on the teaching of St Paul, who urged the restive Roman Christians to do as they were told by the civil power, since "all authority came from God." On this foundation, confirmed by Christ's instruction to render unto Caesar what is Caesar's, there was built up a theory of the rightness, and even of the sanctity, of the imperial authority—a theory, of course, in sharp contradiction to the other popular view that the State was a diabolical monstrosity. Nevertheless, the "all-authority-from-God" line of thinking became a strong tradition and was fostered, understandably enough, by all those writers who were concerned to prove that Christians were "loyal".

If the Government was from God, it seemed to follow that what it did in the necessary course of governing was also from God; and an important part of this governing was evidently the punishing of criminals and the policing of the frontiers of the Empire. Consequently, many Christian writers come out clearly in support of judicial punishment, even though they make it clear on other occasions that Christians should have nothing to do with punishment; some even go so far as to approve of the State's use of capital punishment, while they otherwise hold fast to the primitive Christian abhorrence of bloodshed of all kinds.[1]

Such contradictory attitudes could only be tolerated so long as they did not concern closely the conduct of a Christian—so long, that is, as Christians were able to regard themselves as a "specialized" religious community, with a different function from that of "the world" in which they were involved. As long as this was the case they were able to regard themselves in the same way as the celibate religious orders of later times, who never had to concern themselves with the problem, "What if everyone did as we do?" But for the early Christians this state of affairs did not last; as Christianity became more and more integrated with society, as there was increasing pressure on magistrates to become Christians and on Christians to become magistrates, on soldiers to become Christians, and on Christians to become soldiers, so the problem of reconciling the way of Christ with the way of the world became more and more central.

Early in the fourth century, the Roman Emperor Constantine the Great made Christianity the official religion of the Empire. State and Church entered into a rather premature marriage which, if it did not quite work out as Constantine expected, nevertheless had a profound influence on the whole subsequent development of Western religious thought. At once, the enemies of the Church became the enemies of the State. Paganism and superstition were suppressed as Christianity had been a little while before; and Constantine himself entered energetically into the "battle" against heresy, using the sword of the flesh as well as the sword of the spirit.

St Augustine, the intellectual giant who did more than any other writer to shape the future patterns of Western thought, wrote at the end of the fourth and the beginning of the fifth centuries, when the marriage between State and Church was already more than half a century old. He wrote, that is, as the intellectual champion of a Church allied to the State and co-extensive with the Empire; and he wrote at a time when there had been Christians in the army for about two hundred years, and their presence had been increasingly accepted *de facto* as normal. What is more, he wrote from a position of close political involvement. In his time, the Roman Empire was attacked both in Europe and in Africa by the Vandals, whose activities, whether real or imaginary, are commemorated in our modern word "vandalism", and most of their "vandalism" was directed against the institutions of the Roman Church. In these circumstances, St Augustine was asked to give his opinions about military service; and he was not asked "in the abstract" by theology students, but very much "in the concrete", by individuals in perplexing situations. He was asked, for instance, by a general of the Roman forces in Africa, when Africa was threatened by a Vandal invasion, whether it would not be a good thing to leave the army and go into a monastery; and he was asked, above all, to reply to charges of "disloyalty" against the Christians in this time of great national peril.

It is hardly surprising that there emerged out of this situation, from the pen of an African bishop, the first authoritative teaching that a man can serve in the army and also serve God.

2. PERSISTENCE OF THE EARLY TRADITION IN ST AUGUSTINE

It is remarkable evidence of the way the early tradition of pacifism lasted that St Augustine was called upon to say whether a man could serve in the army and be a Christian, and to answer charges of disloyalty, after more than fifty years of intimate union between Church and State. Even more striking, however, is the obvious persistence of the early tradition in the mind of St Augustine himself, and the tensions which resulted when he tried to reconcile this early tradition with the ruling about military service which he felt bound to make.

Most people today would say that war can obviously

be justified on the principle of self-defence. A person clearly has a right to live, and from that it follows, equally clearly, that he has a right to defend his life against violent and unjust attack. If an individual can do this with his fists or with a gun, why should a group not be able to do it with an army, or even with a nuclear bomb? Just as the individual would normally be expected to preserve his life like this in a lawless land, so a country would be expected to defend itself like this in an internationally lawless world. No doubt but that the act of defence would mean, in extreme cases, killing the aggressor, and this would be legitimate for the group as for the individual.

The extraordinary thing is that St Augustine, who founded the just-war tradition in Christian thought, not only did not argue like this, but would certainly have denied that this argument had any validity at all; and his main reason would have been that its first premise is untrue, for an individual Christian has *no right to kill in self-defence.*

The point is made quite explicitly at the beginning of a little treatise on freewill.[2] The thing that makes sin sinful, according to St Augustine, is *libido*—that is, an excessive attachment to transitory things; and transitory things are those things which can be taken from us against our wills—not spiritual things like wisdom, but worldly things like life, liberty, and honour. To kill in order to defend transitory things is obviously to show an undue attachment to them, and therefore to commit sin, according to the definition. St Augustine knows, of course, that you cannot base any laws on this kind of ideal, and he wants to make room for sensible laws; so he makes a subtle accommodation, saying that it might be a good *law* to permit killing in self-defence, since this is, from the State's point of view, just permitting the lesser of two evils, from the objective point of view of the State—the death of the bad man, the attacker, rather than the death of the good man, who is attacked. All the same, he goes on, good law or not, to permit killing in self-defence is not to *enforce* it, and a Christian could never be excused for committing such an obviously sinful act.

Whatever its philosophical wrappings, there is no doubt that this very rigorous view of the limits of self-defence has much to do with the scriptural command to "resist not evil", and it shows how closely one half of St Augustine's mind was with the early Church. It was a favourite theme of his sermons that enemies were to be loved—and that this was the one commandment that no-one could get out of. We may be exempt from almsgiving, because we have no money to give; but no Christian could claim to be exempt from loving his enemies, because he had no love to give.[3] We can even find in St Augustine's sermons the rather odd view that we should love our enemies *more* than our friends, for the very logical reason that our friends may flatter and pamper us, and so bring us nearer to eternal damnation, whereas our enemies, by making us suffer, give us an invaluable opportunity to come nearer to the Kingdom of God.[4]

Above all, the doctrine of the spiritual kingdom, opposed to the worldly kingdom, is paramount in all St Augustine's thinking. The main theme of the *City*

2+

of God is the contrast between these two kingdoms. The worldly kingdom is filled with strife and bitterness, attacked by enemies within and without, its rulers thinking themselves conquerors of nations when they are in reality only the slaves of vices, exulting in victory when they should rather be grieving over sorrows to come.[5] In moving language, Augustine extols the fortitude of the first Christians who died as martyrs to bear witness to the eternal joys of the Kingdom of God, whereas if God had wished that they should fight, they would have been so numerous that nothing could have resisted them.[6] They followed, he said, the example of Christ himself, who also suffered death willingly in order to bring home to men the greater reality of the spiritual kingdom.

Not only was St Augustine very close to the mind of the first "protesters" against war in these respects, but he spoke with bitter and personal knowledge of the horror of war as a great human tragedy, and of the waste and destruction which it involved. He does not spare to attack the martial spirit of Rome on these occasions; after all, he was himself an African, a member of a subject race, and nowhere does he speak with greater feeling than when he is describing the Punic Wars, which Rome waged against the African city of Carthage. In language that seems surprisingly modern he describes how the two powerful nations were "straining every nerve and using all their resources against one another; how many smaller kingdoms were crushed, how many large and flourishing cities were demolished, how many states were overwhelmed and ruined, how many districts and lands far and near were desolated!"[7]

Quite in harmony with the early Church, he connects these wars with the diabolical powers who are always working for man's destruction; he observes that certain idolatrous games were renewed in Rome as the wars progressed, and he has no doubt that these celebrations were echoed in hell, where there must have been great sport and rejoicing among the devils at the abundance of disastrous quarrels, bloody victories, and dying men.[8] It is to St Augustine, too, that we owe the comparison of kingdoms without international justice to organized bands of robbers, and the suggestion that Alexander the Great was nothing other than a large-scale international crook.[9]

There is, in fact, so much lively anti-war writing in St Augustine that he has been mined just as often by pacifists as by anti-pacifists in their search for traditional ammunition to help them in their debates.

3. THE UNEASY RECONCILIATION

In spite of all this, there is not the slightest doubt that Augustine did teach, clearly and consistently, that a man could be a Christian and a Roman soldier. What is interesting for us is the way he tried to reconcile this with the kind of spirituality that had made the early Christians renounce all carnal warfare.

The first problem is how one can love one's enemies and also do them violence, how one can suffer injury gladly and at the same time retaliate, forgive injuries and at the same time punish the offender—in other words, the whole question of fitting the Sermon on the Mount into the scheme of a "just war".

The question is dealt with at length in a letter which Augustine wrote to a friend, Marcellinus,[10] who was troubled by criticism that the Christian was bound to be disloyal if he followed the teaching of Christ. Augustine takes the problem very seriously; that is, he does not for a moment try to undervalue the importance of "not to render evil for evil", nor does he suggest that it is less relevant for nations than for individuals. Indeed, he goes so far with this line of thought that he conjures up the possibility of a kind of "non-violent imperialism". What is a republic, he asks, but a commonwealth, and what is a commonwealth but people living together *in concord*?—that very concord which is fostered above all by the precepts of forgiveness and non-retaliation. He even attributes Caesar's success to his disposition to forget wrongs and injuries; and he concludes: "If our religion were listened to as it deserves, it would establish, consecrate, and enlarge the commonwealth in a way beyond all that Romulus, Numa, Brutus and all the other men of renown in Roman history achieved." In spite of all this, room must be made for military service; and it is made, not by undervaluing the precepts, but by revaluing them in political terms. The point Augustine makes is that the precepts of patience are always binding; they bind us to an interior disposition of the heart, a benevolence which will always work against the spirit of retaliation; but they do not necessarily bind us to any particular *external act*—as is evident from the example of Christ himself, who did not turn the other cheek to those who struck it, but asked, "Wherefore strikest thou me?" Now it is clear, the argument goes on, that our very love and desire for the welfare of others can be expressed in actions which are against their wishes, and which cause them pain—such as when a stern but loving father corrects his son. By analogy, even the wars of the commonwealth could be carried on directly in order to bring the benefits of peace, piety and order to the resisting state.

The same distinction between the internal and the external action is used when St Augustine has to explain how God could possibly have started the wars of the Old Testament, and how the Prophets and Patriarchs could have taken part in them.[11] The precepts of the Sermon on the Mount, he explains, are binding only in the soul, the *sanctum cubile* of virtue —not in the outward acts of the body—and in this sense, the Patriarchs obeyed them. He does not follow up this line of thought, however, for it is not easy to reconcile the wars in question with a disposition to "turn the other cheek", however secret and "inward". Instead, he suggests another way of looking at the Old-Testament wars. In the time of the Patriarchs, the Kingdom of God was wrapped in a cloud, and this cloud was the worldly kingdom of Israel, which had to be maintained by violence; but the New Testament showed that there was a new life, a new kingdom, for which the old was to be scorned.

As the worldly kingdom is to be scorned, it is hard to see how St Augustine could justify killing for it; and this brings us to the second major problem, the second source of tension, in his thought about war. The nearest he ever gets to resolving this tension is when he suggests, on a number of occasions, that the worldly kingdom, for all its transitoriness, has *some* value, that worldly peace is at least *some* kind of peace, that glory won in victorious battle is *some* kind of glory. But his thought is so dominated by the idea of the new spiritual kingdom which Christ has founded, that he never mentions these lesser values without saying how relative they are, how trivial, in comparison with the absolute and eternal values of the Kingdom of God. It is very difficult to see, therefore, how he can justify killing for this brittle kingdom, when he will not on any account allow the individual to kill in order to preserve his own ephemeral life and liberty. This problem remains outstanding in his philosophy; it is never faced so directly as the previous one concerning the precepts of patience.

Another aspect of St Augustine's efforts at accommodation of Scripture to worldly values is the use of "peripheral" texts to limit the scope of the texts on which pacifism was based—texts, that is, which are not really *about* violence or the love of enemies, but which seem to show that there is in the Gospels themselves a kind of acceptance of war, and which therefore "prove" that one must not be too stringent in drawing pacifist conclusions from the central teaching. The centurion, for instance, was commended by Jesus for faith—but he was not rebuked for his profession, or told to leave it. The soldiers who came to John the Baptist were told to be content with their pay and to do no violence—but were not told to leave the army. The texts had been used in this curious way before, of course; but St Augustine gave this use his great authority. He had, in addition, a rather ingenious twist of his own to add to the argument: Jesus had said that we should give to Caesar what was Caesar's, that is, the coin of the tribute; but this very coin was used to provide the soldiers' pay, with which they "had to be content". Clearly, it was *possible* to please God and be a soldier.[12]

Apart from this kind of argumentation, there is little in St Augustine in the way of positive and detailed teaching about the just war, telling us what kinds are just and how we are to distinguish them. His central concern is to resolve the basic moral tensions, to produce some kind of "accommodation"; beyond this, he only has a few more or less disconnected and scattered observations which have since been pieced together and "systematized". Most important of these observations is the often repeated idea that war is always fought *for peace*; even bands of robbers, he says, do not fight for the sake of fighting, but to reach some kind of peace, or order.[13] This idea helps St Augustine to express his basic revulsion against war, his sense of its abnormality, and to make it clear that only the *destruction of war itself* can justify its use. In other places, he seems to think of war mainly as a kind of punishment of, criminals, a way of humbling the proud and arrogant; and it is this idea which later formed the cornerstone of the "just-war" theory. Elsewhere he throws out more detailed suggestions as to what might constitute a "just war", but without committing himself to them; and on the one occasion where he quotes Tully's rules, old unresolved tensions surge up to the surface again. Tully had said that a just war is fought to preserve the "safety" or the "faith" of a city;

but St Augustine wonders whether safety and faith can always be preserved *together* in the earthly city—and says that in the Kingdom of God, safety and faith are one.[14]

It is not a just-war doctrine, but a tension between the world and the Scriptures, that is central in St Augustine; and the "accommodation", such as it is, is always an uneasy one. In spite of his "justification" of war, he writes towards the end of his life: "Let everyone who thinks with pain on all these great evils, so horrible, so ruthless, acknowledge that this is misery; and if anyone either endures or thinks of them without mental pain, his is a more wretched plight still, for he thinks himself happy because he has lost all human feeling." And his last words on the subject are in a letter written to one Darius who has made peace with the Vandals without a battle: "Those who fight, if they are good men, doubtless seek for peace; nevertheless, it is through blood ... It is a higher glory to slay war itself with the Word, than men by the sword, and to maintain peace by peace, rather than by war."

4. A WAY OUT: *DEUS EX MACHINA*

In view of his difficulties, St Augustine sometimes looked for an easy way out; and there was a way ready to hand. If God *himself* can start a war, it must be a just one; and there is plenty of evidence in the Old Testament to show that he did. If he did in the past, why should he not do so again? *Bellum deo auctore* would solve all problems. No need to ask whether the combatants will be filled with love for their enemies, because they will be following the will of God who is the source of all justice and of all love. No need to ask whether it makes sense to fight for the earthly kingdom, because, if we fight at God's orders, then we must obviously be fighting for his kingdom.[15]

This idea of the God-inspired war becomes a very familiar little theme on the periphery of St Augustine's reflections about war, singing to us its graceful invitation to avoid all difficulties and "with it fade away into the forest dim". On at least three occasions, after a few sentences in which he gives his mind to the question of when a war can be called just, he ends by saying how perfectly just and innocent must be those wars begun at the command of God, or with his direct authority; and, although this kind of war, however it happens, is thought of as something different from the ordinary State war, there is a dangerous tendency to bring together the idea of the God-inspired war with the idea that the power of the State comes from God; and the two ideas are then ready to combine in a rather unholy compound.

Just as St Augustine's thoughts concerning the initiation of war tended to swing towards *Bellum deo auctore*, so his thoughts about participation in it tended to swing towards obedience, service, compliance with the right order willed by God, which from the soldier's point of view avoids the whole problem of personal responsibility, just as the other idea does from the point of view of the prince. A soldier may innocently serve even under a sacrilegious emperor; for, unless what is commanded is clearly against the command of

2*

God, the soldier preserves his innocence by the right order of obedience.[16]

So far as the shedding of blood is concerned, since St Augustine cannot accept the idea of an individual killing in his own defence, or on his own behalf, he must say that when a man acts as the servant of authority this completely changes the moral quality of his action—he then acts without *libido*, and is "covered" by obedience; and the prince himself may be without *libido* if he is following the will of God.

It almost seems as if *Bellum deo auctore* and rightful obedience are the only ways that St Augustine can see, intellectually, out of the moral dilemma—a dilemma that he felt all the more intensely because of his sympathy with the early Church and its pacifism. But, by an odd irony of circumstance, he thus foreshadowed in his doctrine the notion of a "holy war", the direct antithesis to the teaching of Christ, which was to erupt as a terrible historical reality seven hundred years later, at the dawn of the Middle Ages.

NOTES

[1] Lactantius, for instance, seems to be in this category. See Cadoux, p. 203.

[2] Augustine, *De Libero Arbitrio* (*PL*, 32, 1227-8).

[3] Augustine, *Sermon 225* (*PL*, 39, 2161).

[4] Augustine, *Sermon 62* (*PL*, 39, 1862).

[5] Augustine, *The City of God*, 15, 4.

[6] Augustine, *Contra Faustum* (*PL*, 42, 449).

[7] Augustine, *The City of God*, 3, 26.

[8] Augustine, *The City of God*, 3, 26.

[9] Augustine, *The City of God*, 4, 4.

[10] Augustine, *Ep. 138* (*PL*, 33, 525-32).

[11] Augustine, *Contra Faustum* (*PL*, 42, 444–9).

[12] Augustine, *Contra Faustum* (*PL*, 42, 447).

[13] Augustine, *The City of God*, 19, 12.

[14] Augustine, *The City of God*, 22, 6.

[15] See for example, *Contra Faustum* (*PL*, 42, 448), *Commentary on the Heptateuch* (*PL*, 42, 444), and *De Libero Arbitrio* (*PL*, 32, 1227–8).

[16] Augustine, *Contra Faustum* (*PL*, 42, 448–9).

[17] Augustine, *De Libero Arbitrio* (*PL* :32, 1227).

3. THE CONSECRATION OF VIOLENCE

IN the year 1095, at the end of the Council of Clermont, the Pope launched a dramatic appeal to the whole of the Western Church to join in a holy war against the new civilization of Islam. This appeal was the beginning of the crusading movement, a traumatic experience for Western civilization, which had a profound and lasting effect on our religious consciousness, and especially on our attitude to war. It was not by any means an adjustment of doctrine to historical necessity, but rather a tremendous coalescence of religion, myth and reality in one huge historical explosion, which is as important to students of history as it is to students of religion. The crusading movement had many roots; and its vitality is a measure of their depth.

War had been officially "justifiable" ever since St Augustine had put the full weight of his authority behind the "just war". But this accommodation was not of very great historical significance. It was, after all, just an adjustment of doctrine on a fairly high intellectual plane to what was in fact the case. Wars, naturally enough, continued to be the case; but what is more significant in the history of Christianity is that the protest of the early Church remained a very living force in the Christian community, because this protest had been a real and formative Christian experience of a much deeper nature than the subsequent "modification". Consequently, Christians who killed in war, whether it was a just war or not, still had to do long periods of penance, officially at least, until well into the eleventh century.[1] The clergy and the religious orders were absolutely forbidden to take any part in war, and they continue in this way, as a new "specialized" community, the original Christian attitude. There were odd saints who happen to be soldiers; but none whose sanctity had any intimate connection with his profession.[2] There was no positive teaching about the "duties" of the soldier's life (apart from the rather uninspiring scriptural teaching to "be content with their pay"); and, of course, there was nothing approaching the idea of the holy Christian knight who later came into the centre of the stage of medieval Christendom.

On the other hand, there was an ever-growing tension, not between the theory of pacifism and the theory of the just war, but rather between the Christian religion of peace and the Germanic religion of war, for the latter formed a very important part of the mental make-up of the primitive races who were rapidly absorbed into Christian culture in the centuries after the break-up of the Roman Empire. In the religion of the Germanic races, as indeed of many primitive peoples, war held pride of place; all the greatest virtues were the virtues of the warrior, the gods were the gods of war, and death on the battlefield was the warrior's martyrdom. In the tenth century there was a great infusion of North-Germanic blood into Christendom when the Normans descended on the coasts of northern

Europe and later gained a foothold in Sicily and Italy. The Normans were not far removed from their primitive ancestors; though they very rapidly "adopted" Christianity, Wotan, the god of war, still raged in their blood, if not in their minds. It is not just a coincidence that they are connected in many ways with the growth of the crusading ideal.

Some fusion of the religion of war and the religion of peace had already taken place long before the Crusades. On the mythological plane, many of the activities of Wotan were transferred to the archangel Michael, the leader of the heavenly hosts in the Christian tradition. Churches were dedicated to Michael in places once sacred to Wotan, and a "St Michael's Mass" was initiated to secure victory in war[3]; in this way the old tradition of the war against demons was linked up more and more with material battles. The ideals of Christianity and battle heroism came very close together in the first Anglo-Saxon saint, Oswald, and in Charlemagne, the eighth-century founder of "Christian Europe". Charlemagne lived by the sword, and in his conquests was considered the servant of the Church. He fought with all the pomp and circumstance of the ancient Israelites. Just as Jahweh, the Lord of Hosts, presided over their battles, so St Peter, the patron of the Franks, presided over his; in the place of their prophets stood the Frankish bishops who prayed for victory, and the holy relics were carried into battle just as the Israelites carried the Ark of the Covenant. Germanic traditions blended well with the themes of the Old Testament.[4]

All the same, this was still not the full consecration

of militarism which was to come later. Wars were
decorated with all the trappings of religion, and Church
and State were in harmony; but these were not exactly
holy wars, with Christianity as the main driving force;
and, even if the office of king was holy, the profession
of the individual soldier was not yet thought of as a
way of sanctity. Above all, there was, right until the
eleventh century, an unresolved conflict between the
tradition of the Church and any tradition which could
glorify an act of killing.

The best evidence of this conflict comes from the
popular lives of the saints, which reflect the shifting
ideals of heroism in society. One of these is the *Life
of Edmund*, King of East Anglia,[5] which tries to combine the ideals of Christian martyr and the battle-chief,
with intriguing results. Edmund has to face a Viking
invasion of his territory; the marauding bands treacher-
ously and secretly steal into his country, kill most of
his people, take him by surprise in a village and scorn-
fully demand, through a messenger, that he should
become their vassal, and pay them tribute. Edmund's
bishop, who happens to be with him, advises sub-
mission or flight, since resistance would be useless. It
is at this point that Edmund comes to life as a true
battle-hero, speaking the traditional words and echoing
the traditional sentiments. Nothing could be more
despicable in the heroic tradition than the two policies
recommended by the Bishop; defiantly, Edmund re-
fuses either to flee or to submit, and he flings back the
Vikings' scorn into the teeth of the messenger, saying
that he would kill him there and then but that he could
not bear the thought of defiling his pure hands in such

foul blood. This is no Christian abhorrence of blood-shed; it is rather the aristocratic warrior's refusal to dabble in blood of an inferior stock! But then comes the odd part of the story; Edmund *throws away* his weapons. The shock is not quite so great as it might have been, because it has been made clear that resistance would be useless from the military point of view; but all the same, it is an odd thing to do, in the heroic tradition, which always holds fast to the idea that it is better to go down fighting. From this point onwards, Edmund comes out of his heroic chrysalis as the *traditional Christian martyr*, at least in external behaviour, his suffering and death very closely modelled on the suffering and death of Christ—though in Edmund's case one cannot help feeling that it is his *defiance* of the enemy rather than his love of them that he is expressing by his endurance! The story is evidently rather a *tour de force* in the history of heroic ideals; and it is hardly surprising that later versions of the Edmund story resolve the tensions by making him a very straightforward martyr, getting rid altogether of the heroic side of his behaviour and language, and even making him into a kind of hero of non-violence, who, after much bloodshed, is converted from his trust in war and resolves never more to fight the barbarians, but to put on instead the spiritual armour of Christ.[6]

St Gerald of Aurillac is even more odd, and even more ambitious.[7] He too is a feudal lord, though not a king, and he must sometimes fight to defend his poor people against scoundrels. He fights heroically, and always wins; but there is something very curious about his tactics. He always orders his men to charge with their spears and swords *backwards*, presumably so that they won't hurt anyone. A command like this, the pious biographer remarks, would not have been obeyed in ordinary circumstances; but these soldiers do as they are told, since they know that "Gerald always wins". Once again, as with Origen and Augustine, *Deus ex machina* is brought in to resolve a difficult moral dilemma.

Even on the eve of the Crusades the dilemma is still a pressing one. A story is told of a pilgrimage to Jerusalem which was set upon by Bedouin robbers; the pilgrims decide to defend themselves by arms, to "ensure their salvation"—but after two days of fighting a priest is overcome by remorse, and denounces the pilgrims for trusting in themselves instead of in God, with the result that they abandon their weapons and start to pray, and end up by arranging an armistice with the Arabs.[8]

2. THE LIVING MYTH

The Crusades put an end to this kind of difficulty; but we can only really understand how they did this by trying to understand the extraordinary vitality of the original movement.

In two ways, Pope Urban the Second, who launched the first appeal, saw the Crusades as a "healing war"— a war for unity. In the first place, it was to heal the wound which had separated the Eastern Church from the Western for centuries and which had divided Christendom into two great power blocs, centred on Rome and Constantinople. By going to help the

Emperor in the East against the common foe of all Christendom, the Christians of the West would forge a new bond of union with him. Beyond this lay the dream of the Land of Promise, the Old Jerusalem mysteriously merged with the New, where a Church renewed in holiness and in unity would bear the burden of the Last Days, and await the second coming of Christ.[9]

Urban's words flew among the peoples of Europe like sparks among stubble, and within months the whole countryside was ablaze with enthusiasm. The Pope himself toured and preached, the bishops spread his message; and numerous "holy men", of whom Peter the Hermit is the best remembered, spread the "good news" with their peculiar zeal. "The word of God", wrote one of the bishops, "was scattered plentifully, and every day increased the number of "Jerusalemites"; those who stayed were ashamed, and those who were preparing to leave gloried of it publicly. Everyone encouraged his neighbour, and eager discussions went on in public places, at the street corners and at the crossroads."[10]

It was not just the prosperous and well-equipped mounted warriors who set out on the gruelling three-thousand-mile trek right across Europe, down through the deserts of Asia Minor, down through Syria into Palestine; it was also the peasants and artisans, the poor and the needy, who flocked to the standards. In any village street men could be seen loading their trivial belongings on to carts, hitching these to their oxen, and lumbering off with their wives and families to the Land of Promise. The children, soon weary of the journey, and doomed never to return, asked anxiously whenever they saw a strange castle or town, "Is *that* Jerusalem?"[11]

How can we account for this tremendous wave of crusading enthusiasm?

The years immediately before the First Crusade were brimful of internal violence in Western Christendom. In 1066 the Normans, with the Pope's blessing, conquered Christian Britain, exterminated the English nobility, and destroyed the whole population in rebellious districts, until their mastery over the country was complete. In Italy a predecessor of Urban's, who was known as "Hildebrand" ("Battlesword"), was for many years at war with the Holy Roman Emperor, Henry IV of Germany; four times the papal forces had been besieged in Rome, and the streets of the holy city had flowed with Christian blood, shed by their Christian foes. Everywhere petty wars were carried on by feudal lords anxious to enlarge their petty dominions.

The Church had tried to control war by the "Truce of God" which protected certain holy days and certain holy people from acts of violence; but the disease was too radical to respond readily to such first-aid. If violence is hard to suppress, however, it is not so hard to *divert*. Urban offered to his quarrelsome Christian leaders the prospect of unlimited conquest in new lands, conquest sanctioned by the highest moral authority; let them cease to tear each other to pieces, disputing over their share of a limited area of land, and march side by side in the name of Christ against the pagans.

This may account for the appeal of the Crusade

to the leaders; but it hardly accounts for its appeal to the common people. To understand this, we have to explore the wonderland of legend and myth. The people were possessed by a vision, which we can see gradually forming in signs and wonders and legends which gathered around the first expedition. The centre of the vision was the new Kingdom of Jerusalem, in which the new People of God were to make their eternal home, and wait for the final attack of the forces of Antichrist, which would in turn herald the second coming of Jesus in glory to take possession of his kingdom. The new myth had deep roots; it revived the age-old dream of the kingdom of Charlemagne, the King of France who, two centuries before, had been crowned Emperor of Christendom, and had ruled over an extensive European kingdom; and this myth itself had even deeper roots because Charlemagne was considered as the heir both of imperial Rome and of the heaven-born kings of the ancient Franks, from whom he was descended. Although Charlemagne's kingdom fell to pieces very soon after his death, his name rapidly passed into legend, and he was one of the founder-figures of the "united Christendom" of the Middle Ages. The Crusade looked towards a new Christendom, which would fulfil the promise of Charlemagne, and which would be ruled over by the "last King of the Franks", Carolus Redivivus, who, according to pro-phecy, was to play a decisive part in the Last Days. The whole history of the emergence of Christian civili-zation out of chaos was embodied in this great popular myth, which seemed to give a vital meaning to world history.

The great hope dawned in a great darkness. The years before the Crusade were filled with uncontrollable natural disasters as well as wars for the people of Western Europe. Floods, droughts and plagues ravaged the countryside, and populations were decimated by the mysterious "burning disease" which caused terrible disfigurement before death, and which looked like an awful "judgement of God". It needs a great effort of the imagination for us to have an insight into the horror of those times when crowded populations were completely at the mercy of disease and elemental disaster.

It would, however, be false to regard the First Crusade as an escape from the "scourges", and to underestimate the tremendous surge of religious fervour which accompanied the disasters. Though encouraged by Church reform, this was more than anything else a surging of the common people, aware of new possibilities of endeavour, and intensely concerned with communal life, communal work and worship. The prophets of the movement were typically the hermits, holy men and oracles of the people, only on the "fringe" of the Church establishment; on a wave of religious enthusiasm people went flooding into religious orders, but the same enthusiasm later gave us our first great cathedrals, built by great penitential work-camps.

This was the stubble which was set on fire by the words of Pope Urban II; here was a chance for the people not only to leave behind for good all distress, disease and unhappiness but actually to do something communally to "help on" the Kingdom of God, to begin to build here and now the New Jerusalem, which they would one day see with their own eyes.

When they set off, the crusaders bound themselves by a solemn oath not to desert the cause; and in return they had the papal promise of a plenary indulgence if they should die on the Crusade. So to set off on this adventure was, one way or another, to set off for heaven. No wonder the departure was accompanied by all manner of signs and wonders—battles in the sky, miraculous migrations of insects and miraculous "stigmata" on the flesh of the crusaders.

In such a mood a representative section of the people of Christendom, after a thousand years of uneasy accommodation to the world's violence, set off on an expedition to the land of Jesus to carry out a mission which was the most flagrant violation of his teaching—to build the Kingdom of God by the sword.

3. The Myth in Practice

The immediate historical consequences of the Crusades need not detain us long; there are few people left who regard them as "glorious", apart from the romantic and ill-informed. Nothing could teach us more clearly that violence is a treacherous servant.

As the popular hordes moved across Europe they began their apocalyptic adventure by murdering or forcibly "baptizing" the Jewish communities who were unfortunate enough to come in their way. This was because the conversion of the Jews was part of the prophecies of the Last Days.

When they eventually arrived at Constantinople,

they were given a very doubtful welcome by the Emperor, who wanted mercenary soldiers to defend his kingdom, not religious enthusiasts inspired by the idea of a "holy war". However, they were ferried across the Bosphorus in due course and made their way down into Syria, where their Norman leaders immediately settled down to carve out private kingdoms for themselves, forgetting that their destination was the Holy City. There the story might have ended, had not the enthusiasm of the common people carried their leaders on almost forcibly to Jerusalem, which was eventually sacked and plundered by the Christian force.

In this way the Kingdom of Jerusalem was founded. The forces of Islam soon mustered, however, against the occupying power, and the remaining Crusades were little more than a protracted effort to force back the rising tide of Moslem power. Within a century the Kingdom of Jerusalem fell; later still, Constantinople itself fell, and Islam advanced far into Europe. The enmity between the two civilizations endured, and the tide of conquest did not turn decisively in favour of "Christendom" until technical advances in the nineteenth century enabled Britain and France to found their colonial empires in the territories of Mohammed. The sorry legacies of these empires are still with us.

The effect of the Crusades on Christian unity was a masterpiece of historical irony. They were intended to heal the wounds which separated East from West but they ended by deepening these wounds and confirming a fierce hostility within the Christian Church which has lasted now for nearly nine hundred years. From the beginning, the Emperor of Constantinople had been suspicious of these vast and ill-disciplined armies, not only because of their religious fanatics, but because they could so easily turn against him and build their own empires for themselves from the remnants of his. His first step therefore was to extract an oath of allegiance from the leaders of the hosts as they arrived in his kingdom, pledging them to restore to him all the lands they reconquered from the Turks. He then let them proceed through his territories, but not without dogging their progress with his own troops, in order to prevent plundering.

The Emperor's suspicions were of course very fully justified, as was subsequently proved by the behaviour of the crusading chiefs, who kept land for themselves in spite of their oaths. All the same, these suspicions could not but aggravate the suspicions of the Crusaders themselves; and, in the bitter campaigns which followed, the Western Christians made the Emperor and his Greek subjects their scapegoats, blaming every setback on to their treachery.

This prepared the way for the great tragedy of the Fourth Crusade, when an expedition which set out to recapture Palestine was diverted by Venetian subtlety, into a war against Constantinople. Just over a hundred years after the First Crusade, Christians of the West sacked and looted the capital city of the Christians of the East, and wantonly destroyed the priceless treasures of Greek culture. In this way a Latin Empire was founded in Constantinople and the Latin liturgy was heard in St Sophia. The Empire was short lived; but not so the hatred which was engendered by the holy war for Christian unity.

4. HOLY VIOLENCE

What finally overwhelmed the early Christian protest against violence was not, then, a just-war theory, but a more powerful fanaticism of war. *Militia Christi*, the "soldiers of Christ", a term once used to contrast the life of the Christian fighting for a spiritual kingdom with the life of the pagan Roman soldier, comes to mean simply a soldier who specializes in fighting Moslems.

The coming together of violence and holiness is reflected at all levels of the Church's life. In the wonder-working popular imagination, its most powerful and most horrifying symbol is the Holy Lance.[12] This was the spear with which the Roman soldier pierced the side of Christ after the Crucifixion—for the early Christians a symbol at once of ultimate human cruelty and of the sacrificial love of Christ which suffered this cruelty for our redemption. When the armies of the First Crusade were particularly hard pressed in Antioch, they "discovered" this lance hidden in the Church of St Peter. Carried point foremost, the Holy Lance then led the Christian armies to Jerusalem, where they plundered all the houses and public buildings, and murdered men, women and children until, according to the chronicles, "the horses were up to their knees in blood". The Holy Lance had changed its function in the popular imagination.

At the same time, in the liturgy of the Church, ceremonies spring up which express the newly discovered sanctity of war[13]—the blessing of standards, the blessing of weapons, the consecration of knights—ceremonies which very often are a continuation of age-old pagan rites. From the eleventh century comes the blessing for a newly girded sword—"Bless, O Lord, Almighty Father, by the invocation of thy holy name, and by the coming of thy son Jesus Christ, and by the gift of the Holy Spirit, this sword, that he who girds it today in piety may crush all his enemies underfoot, and in all things should forever be prosperous and victorious." The Roman Pontifical still has a "Blessing for a new soldier" from the same century, and in much the same spirit.

War now became a way of holiness for the laity, just as the monastic life was for the "religious", and in this way partly met the aspiration towards a new kind of lay holiness which was part of the religious ferment of the eleventh century. "God has established in our time the Holy War", writes a contemporary, "so that the knights and lay folk who spill their blood in battle against the heathen can have a new way to salvation. They need not go into a monastery nor renounce the world by vows, but they can win God's grace in their laymen's clothes and in their accustomed freedom."[14]

The culmination of all this development was the foundation, in the Christian Kingdom of Jerusalem, of a new religious order, the Knights Templars, who took up residence near the Temple of Solomon, and bound themselves by solemn vows to fight against the enemies of God in poverty, chastity and obedience. Thus, for a short while, the way of violence and the way of monastic perfection were united, and formed one of the high peaks of aspiration for religious enthusiasm.

5. THE DIABOLICAL FOE

When violence becomes sacred, the enemy becomes diabolical; it is hard to say which of these two ideas is the cart and which is the horse, but certain it is that they belong together—it is a necessity of myth. If bloodshed was sacred for the Crusaders it was because their enemies were the enemies of God. If the conquest of Jerusalem was the building of the Kingdom of God, what could the Moslems be but the forces of Antichrist, dimly foreshadowed in the Apocalypse? And so the archetypal image of the "barbaric hordes", which always slumbers in the subconscious, was brought well to the fore once for all in the religious consciousness of Christendom.

Once the idea of the diabolical foe is firmly planted, it is used to interpret every historical event—and it may even begin to shape history.

We can see this happening in Spain during the early years of the crusading myth. The Spaniards were often at war during the eleventh century with invaders from North Africa, just as they were also often at war with each other. Their country was divided into a number of little kingdoms and fights were more or less continuous—sometimes Christians would be opposed to the "Saracens" from Africa, but just as often they would be opposed to other Christians and allied to Saracens, according to the ambitions of particular princes and the state of the *mêlée*. Towards the end of the century, however, they were joined in their battles by ardent French knights, who had quite a different view of the situation, and were inspired with the great dream of Holy Christendom opposed to the demons of the outer darkness. This vision was quite foreign to the realities of the situation; but nevertheless it was a vision of transforming power, and it changed the course of history.

It was not by chance that these enthusiastic knights came from France, the ancient kingdom of Charlemagne, the cradle of Christian Europe. For the material battle against the forces of evil must be carried on in the name of a material and visible Kingdom of God on earth—and where should that be but "Christendom", of which France was the heart?

The enemies within Christendom were to be suppressed as ruthlessly as the enemies without; and the enemies within were heretics. There is a close link between the crusades against the external infidel, the crusades against the internal heretics and the final establishment of the Inquisition, which sought out people accused of heretical "fifth-column" work in the Kingdom of God, and committed to purification by fire—a "judicial" procedure which is perhaps the most terrifying denial of human rights in the history of our civilization. But the "enemy" has no rights against the Church of God, or against Christendom; and in the same way, the enemies without, the Moslems, were without rights against the People of God—no need to debate whether there was a just title to land or a just title to war; the justice of God, as St Augustine had observed, is not to be disputed.

The Crusades gave a characteristic note to the Middle Ages, which was a vital formative period for our civilization; consequently they are still a potent force, especially where Christianity is still dominated by medieval patterns of thought.

NOTES

[1] According to Schmitz, *Bussdisziplin,* forty days' penance is normally prescribed.

[2] The point is discussed by Erdmann, *Die Entstehung des Kreuzzugs-Gedankens,* Stuttgart (1935), pp. 11-12.

[3] The point is fully discussed in Erdmann, p. 18.

[4] Erdmann, p. 20.

[5] A number of versions of the story of King Edmund are brought together in Lord Francis Harvey's *A Garland of St. Edmund.* The Old English version is available in the Early English Text Society edition (ed. Sweet), and in Sweet's *Anglo-Saxon Primer;* the original Latin of Abbo in *PL,* 134, 507-20.

[6] As, for instance, in Lydgate's version, quoted by Harvey.

[7] Odo, *Vita Sancti Geraldi (PL,* 133, 939ff.).

[8] Alphandéry, *La Chrétienté et l'Idée de Croisade,* p. 27.

[9] Alphandéry, pp. 50ff.

[10] *PL,* 166, 1064.

[11] Quoted by Alphandéry, p. 66.

[12] For full story of the Lance see Alphandéry, pp. 99ff.

[13] Details of benedictions in Erdmann, pp. 326-35.

[14] Quoted by Erdmann, p. 311.

PART 2

4. THE PROTEST HUMANIZED

1. The End of Christendom: War and the Nation-States

THROUGHOUT the Middle Ages, the moral question of war slumbered in the conscience of Christendom. The arch-enemy, the heathen Turk, or, in more general terms, the whole of the Moslem world, was always there in the background, and against him it was always good to fight. Within Christendom wars continued much as they had done before the Crusades, and inter-state wars gave birth to civil wars, much as the inter-civilization wars launched by Urban had given birth to East-West wars within Christendom. Nevertheless, the dream of a holy united Christendom continued to hover in men's minds; and because of this, the internal wars of Christendom were always to be regretted, just as the external wars were to be glorified. The Church tried to limit these internal wars by the "Truce of God". The idea of this was to prohibit violence on certain holy days, or against certain holy people, or in certain holy places. The Truce-of-God movement made use of the united faith of Christendom in the interests of peace, and it was certainly the most successful peace-making effort of the medieval Church; but it had to do with practice rather than with theory, with the containment of violence rather than the theology of war.

War itself was not a matter for serious theological

dispute. A stream of eccentric pacifist thought was
continued by small sects, and the religious orders continued the early traditions of non-violence in practice
—to such an extent that it was often stated that the
first condition of a just war was that it should be fought
by laymen. The "official" theory, however, was taken
care of by the just-war tradition, which was gleaned
from St Augustine, put into a kind of legal form by
Gratian in the twelfth century, and repeated with
scholastic clarity by Thomas Aquinas in the thirteenth.[1] The only thing that is surprising about this
tradition in the Middle Ages is how little of it there is.
Thomas Aquinas has only one short question on war
in his *Summa*, compared with twenty-four long ones
about angels! Evidently there was no very serious
problem here for medieval thinkers as there had been
for earlier generations of Christians.

Meanwhile, the traditions of chivalry, inseparable
from the crusading wars, were quietly growing and
exerting a powerful influence, both for good and for
evil, on the emerging hero-ideal of Western culture.
In the *Canterbury Tales*, Chaucer puts a knight among
his pilgrims as the natural leader, and as an embodi-
ment of all that is graceful and noble in the conduct
of a lay aristocrat. He is full of "truthe and honour,
fredom and curteisye", and he is indeed a "verray
parfit, gentil knight". It is however a curious fact that
the one substantial activity of his life is fighting; his
whole adult life has been spent "riding out" on crusading wars, and killing the heathen in various parts of the
world. In this way war and violence are gradually
woven into the very texture of Christian idealism.

Then, at the beginning of the Renaissance, this slumbering period came to an end, and the glory of medieval Christendom finally exploded into a galaxy of little Christendoms, the great national monarchies, from which the pattern of modern Europe began to emerge.

The new pattern had been prepared in the centuries before; but it crystallized during the early sixteenth century in the reign of the three monarchs who occupied the triple pinnacle of European power, Henry VIII of England, Francis I of France, and Charles V, who combined the thrones of Spain and Germany. The intense rivalry of these three cut right across the old pattern in which holy Christendom was lined up against diabolical heathendom. When Francis found himself surrounded by Charles, he corrected the balance of power by making an alliance with the arch-enemy, the Turkish hordes themselves; and when the Pope appealed to the three monarchs to call a truce and join together with him to repel the very real threat of advancing Islam, Cardinal Wolsey replied on behalf of Henry that Englishmen knew no Turks other than the ones who lived just over the Channel—and suggested politely that the Pope should look after himself.[2]

It was not just new political groups which emerged from medieval Christendom but it was new centres of "divine" authority and power. The birth of the little English Christendom is celebrated by Shakespeare in the history plays, which trace the origin of the divinely chosen and protected Tudor monarchy. Henry VIII, as it happens, did actually found a national Church, the Church of England, of which he made

himself the anointed head; but the kings of France
and Spain had just the same ambitions and might well
have done the same had they not found it convenient
at a certain point to ally themselves with the Papacy
—it is only by accident, in this sense, that we have not
a "Church of Spain" and a "Church of France" as well
as a "Church of England". The new monarchies each
inherited something of the glory and splendour of the
ancient myth; and with it they inherited something of
the religion of violence which had been woven into
the fabric of medieval Christendom—only now, the
enemy was the other little Christendoms, and not the
Moslems. Wolsey was speaking more profoundly than
he knew when he said that he knew no Turks but
the French.

A prodigious development in the techniques of war
coincided with the rise of the national monarchies. The
discovery of gunpowder, and the rapid development
of its uses, opened up a whole vista of new possibilities,
which were at once horrifying and fascinating. It gave
rise to the new science of ballistics and to new modes
of fortification. These new techniques, and all the
other arts of war, joined in with the vigorous current
of Renaissance thought to produce a striking fusion of
culture and violence. Guns were objects of beauty;
fortifications became a normal part of town planning
and were an object of civic pride. War is a dominant
theme of literature and a central topic of polite con-
versation; an Italian writer lists the military topics
which are suitable for after-dinner discussion—Why
do women shrink from war? Does the power of an
army consist in planning, leadership, or the valour of

the soldiers? Why do soldiers go so gladly to so perilous a destiny?[3] Title-pages of books are embellished with smoking cannons and miscellaneous engines of war, and tombs of famous men boil over with military ornaments.[4]

At the same time the traditions of chivalry were revitalized. Caxton printed the stories of King Arthur and his knights to inspire men with a vision of the "golden age" of chivalry—which is in fact as hard to trace as the end of a rainbow. Each nation writes its own semi-mythical warlike history, and in England Crecy, Poitiers and Agincourt, the sites of English victories in the notorious Hundred Years' War, become magical symbols. The military virtues of courage, obedience and fortitude are lauded to the skies, and jousts, tournaments and pageants become the order of the day with the monarchs and aristocrats of the new Europe.

2. THE OPPOSITION, IN THE NAME OF HUMANITY AND THE NEW LEARNING

The cult of war did not grow without vigorous opposition; and the most eloquent of its opponents were the group of humanist scholars who wrote at the beginning of the sixteenth century. They were led by four great men who in many ways link the Middle Ages with the modern world: St Thomas More, Henry VIII's friend and sometime chancellor; Erasmus the Dutchman, Vives the Spanish philosopher and Colet, the revolutionary Dean of St Paul's.

These four men had much in common, in spite of

their varied nationalities. They were, to begin with, tied together by bonds of mutual friendship and respect; and the international nature of their scholarly friendship was at once part of the glory of dying Christendom, and a foretaste of the universality of modern science. They were all men of lively sensitivity, vibrating with the excitement of expanding knowledge, as are the great thinkers of our generation; and together with this enlargement of knowledge they had a heightened sense of the possibilities of human progress and of man's responsibility for his own destiny. They were all intimately involved in the turbulent political life of their times; and, above all, they all detested war, as the great contradiction of all their wisdom, their sensitivity, and of the aspirations of the whole human race.[5]

Their protest was not just intellectual, or just emotional or just religious. It was rather the protest of the whole human personality against the whole living reality of war as they experienced it; and one very important part of this reality, as they saw it, was the "religion" of chivalry, in which the old Germanic religion of war had been handed down. St Thomas More knew his own king well; he understood his romantic nature, his love of pageantry and chivalric display—and he felt the heavy burden of England's ruinous and savage wars in France. He may not have been so wrong as later writers have thought in his attack on the cult of chivalric romance.

It is mainly in his book *Utopia* that this attack is worked out.[6] The Utopians, who live on a small island, have assumed intelligent responsibility for their own social progress, and, in the course of seventeen hundred years of sociological research and control, they have worked out for themselves a rational and happy order of society. They have decided that man has two wonderful gifts without which he would not be man; one is the gift of reason, and the other the gift of love; the greatest joy and fulfilment of man, therefore, is to live according to reason and in "love" with his fellow men. Unfortunately, there are on the mainland communities of a much more primitive and irrational kind; and among these primitives there are some individuals who have so perverted their great human gifts as to enjoy brutal killing of their fellow men. These are the professional soldiers. Their perversion is such a deep one, since it affects the very basis of their humanity, that they can only be classified as "mad"; moreover, they are so mad that even the Utopians have to regard them as "incurables".

All the same, the Utopians do sometimes have to fight wars to defend the good life, or to protect the rights of one of their citizens. As they abhor war, they are naturally concerned to get it over as quickly as possible with the least loss of worthy lives; and, as force is brutish, and reason is human, they consider it very much nobler to win by guile than by force. Their tactics are therefore peculiar—by chivalric standards. If they were attacked by a fleet, they would probably "translate the beacons", so that the hostile ships would be wrecked; and as soon as they were at war with a foreign state, they would offer in the enemy country fabulously high rewards for anyone who assassinated the leaders—a device which caused endless chaos and confusion on the other side, for the Utopians were rich and always kept their word.

If such devices did not work, the Utopians might be forced to use armies. In that case, they used their great wealth to recruit the "best" mercenary soldiers, whose greed could be relied on to attract them to the Utopian cause. Battles were therefore usually won without the loss of a drop of Utopian blood—and if large numbers of mercenaries on either side were killed in the process, so much the better. It was really a blessed deliverance for humanity—for they were, after all, incurable madmen! Throughout their campaigns, the Utopians kept a close sense of the bond of common humanity which united them to the sane ordinary people of the enemy state, who were always regarded as the victims or dupes of their unscrupulous leaders. Everything possible was done to avoid causing them suffering; and as soon as the war was over, the Utopians' main concern was to restore them to prosperity and to bring to them the benefits of the "good life".

This is not, of course, political philosophy; it is satire, and the job of satire is to attack. What it attacks is clear enough; it is the illusion that there is something ennobling in the clash of violence with violence, something splendid in reducing a state to degradation and misery—in short, some peculiar glory in war. In this attack More is in harmony with all the humanist writers of his time. Romantic heroes, knights who kill ten, twenty, a hundred men and then go off for more feasts of bloodshed, are held up to contempt; Achilles, Alexander, the heroes of the chivalric age, become the great world-robbers they were for St

Augustine. Vives re-tells the story of the pirate captured by Alexander the Great. When the Emperor asked his captive what wickedness made him trouble the whole sea with one galley, the pirate replied, "The same which makes thee trouble the whole earth!"[7]

The corrosive attack on chivalry is part of a larger theme which underlies most of the humanist critique of war; and that is precisely the *inhumanity*, or the bestiality, of the actual act of war, and the degradation of the lives of those who are involved in it. Vives derives the word *bellum* (war) from another Latin word *belua*, which means "a wild beast". This sets the tone of much of the new protest; and, as literary artists, the humanists try to make their points by arousing disgust.

Disgust, first of all, for the brutality of the battlefield. "Imagine", writes Erasmus, "that thou dost behold two hosts of barbarian people, of whom the look is fierce and cruel, and the voice horrible; the terrible and fearful rustling and glistering of their harness and weapons; the unlovely murmur of so huge a multitude; the eyes sternly menacing; the bloody blasts and terrible sounds of trumpets and clarions; the thundering of the guns, no less fearful than thunder, but much more hurtful; the frenzied cry and clamour, the ferocious and mad running together, the outrageous slaughter, the cruel chances of them that flee and of them that are stricken down and slain, the heaps of corpses, the fields flowing with men's blood, the rivers dyed red with it. Verily, this tragedy involves so many mischiefs, that it would abhor a man's heart to speak thereof."[8]

3*

Disgust, then, for the way of life associated with the man of war; and this meant particularly hunting, the traditional sport of the same class which handed on the traditions of chivalry. Blood sports, for the humanists, show the same kind of perversion, and cultivate the same bestial qualities, as war itself; both take an unnatural delight in what is essentially abhorrent to a healthy human being. Henry VIII, of course, adored hunting; and Erasmus was in Rome when the Pope, Julius II, constructed huge arenas for tournaments and bullfights—the same Pope who, the previous year, had celebrated a bloody triumph at the head of his armies in Erasmus's own university city of Bologna. Talking of the noble sport of the man of war, Erasmus writes, "Even the dung of their dogs smells like cinnamon to them ... and what could be so sweet as to see a beast being butchered!"[9]

Disgust, last of all, for the aftermath of war, the sordid reality of the "glorious homecoming". In 1527 Erasmus wrote an imaginary dialogue between a Carthusian monk and a retired soldier. "What spoils have you brought", asks the monk, "for your wife and children?" "Only syphilis," replies the hero, "to infect those who are nearest and dearest to me." But what sort of a soul does he bring back? About as clean, he answers, as a Paris prostitute, or a common house of office.[10]

This is a sufficient sample to give the flavour of the humanists' comment on the cult of war. The ugliness which they portray in words is echoed visually in the grotesque caricatures of the Flemish painter, Hieronymus Bosch.

3. THE HUMANIST VIEW OF THE JUST WAR AND THE SCRIPTURES

It is not surprising that these scholars, who found the revulsion from war written deep in human nature, should join hands with the early Church, and rediscover the primitive meaning of the New Testament.

Dean Colet of St Paul's, the earliest writer of the group, forged the strongest link with the early Church, by undermining the scholastic commentaries on Scripture, and starting a new tradition of scientific biblical criticism, which makes him a founder-figure of modern scripture scholarship. He begins the job of "uncovering" the New Testament in his sermons on the Epistle to the Romans, the letter in which St Paul advised his little Christian community in Rome, among other things, not to upset the Roman magistrates, because they were the ministers of God. This epistle had been made the basis of elaborate commentaries concerning the rights and duties of the State and the justice of war. Colet thinks this is quite out of place. He asks, not only what can we make this document mean, but what did it in fact mean as a whole, and in the real historical setting, for the people to whom it was addressed? Colet's biblical criticism brings him directly back to the pacifism of the early Church.

His principles were followed by later writers, who in the same way insist on the *whole* meaning. Erasmus enjoys himself in his satire *In Praise of Folly* at the expense of those "learned doctors" who have drawn a justification for violence out of Jesus's advice to his disciples to sell their cloaks and buy a sword. Whatever he meant by this, nothing could be more obvious than that he did *not* mean what these doctors take him to mean! For who could suppose that Jesus, "forgetting all that he had taught his disciples about how they should rejoice in persecution, not resist evil, and take no care of bodily needs, should now be so far from forbidding them to go forth with a sword, that he commanded them to get one, though with the sale of their coat—and had rather they should go naked than want a brawling-iron by their sides!" It is also worth observing, Erasmus continues, that "he who so willed the sword to be brought reprehends it a little after and commands it to be sheathed; and that it was never heard that the Apostles used swords and bucklers against the Gentiles, though it is likely they would have done so if Christ had ever intended as the doctors interpret."[11]

So far as the Church's "just-war tradition" is concerned, Erasmus sees it as the result of the Church "swallowing a gobbet of the civil laws"—which are not exactly the same as the laws of Christ. What is worse, once certain wars are declared just, they are immediately proclaimed as "glorious"! And what is the basis of this justice? It is in practice the will of the prince, be he child or idiot; and even a sane man is not likely to judge that his own cause is unjust.[12] There is still substance in these criticisms.

An interesting sidelight is thrown on the function of the Church at this time by one of Erasmus's "dialogues", in which one Hanno ("Stay-at-home") cross-questions the conquering hero Thrasymachus ("Bold-in-Fight"). The cross-questioning uncovers a sordid tale of lust and violence. But Bold-in-Fight argues that he has heard a parson say in the pulpit that it is lawful for every man to live by his trade; butchers are hired to kill beasts—what is wrong with the soldier, who is hired to kill men? The soldier is intensely annoyed with Stay-at-Home for disturbing his peaceful "conscience"—and he promptly goes off to find an easy confessor, to set it to rights again.[13]

In short, the humanists considered that the Church, through its "just-war" tradition, was in fact neglecting the real meaning of Scripture, and prostituting its moral authority to the service of ambitious and bloodthirsty princes.

4. EDUCATION

There is a certain sense of frustration about all the writings of these Renaissance scholars. They had a heavy sense of responsibility, of man's need to shape his own communal destiny; but how could their sense of responsibility be made effective? They were closely involved in politics; but not as we think of this, as responsible members of a democracy. They were involved rather as the executives, counsellors, advisers, instructors of princes, whose will was always supreme. For all his great authority in the State, St Thomas More is sadly aware that if he once sets a foot wrong with Henry his head will roll in the dust—as it eventually did; and, in spite of his great love of peace, he actually found himself asking Parliament to grant money for Henry's futile French wars—because it seemed to be the only thing to do.

As the first "social scientists", however, they were

concerned with the roots of social disorders, and they saw the roots of war in the whole educational environment, of which the cult of chivalry was an important part; and it was precisely as educationalists that they had their greatest chance to act responsibly. Two of the most important books from this pacifist group were written as manuals of instruction for young members of royal families. One was Erasmus's *Education of a Christian Prince*, presented to his young ward Charles Hapsburg, who was later to become the most powerful monarch of Europe. Some years later, Vives was appointed tutor to Princess Mary, the daughter of Henry VIII, and for her he wrote the *Education of a Christian Woman*.

The problem, as they saw it, was to educate the natural peacefulness of the human personality and to avoid contamination with violence during the impressionable years of infancy. Man, the humanists consider, is by nature a loving and rational creature—as the Utopians defined him, he comes into the world "naked, without armour, formed to meekness and poverty and the lovely society of life".[14] Sometimes this idea of natural goodness took the form of a mythical fall from a golden age of reason and harmony into the corruption of violence. What they are all agreed about is the heavy responsibility of educators; for the seeds of gentleness will not grow unless they are cultivated, and violence is like a blight, a vile and infectious disease which can fester in the imagination and corrupt the whole personality. The woman who occupies her thoughts with tourneys and armour and men's valiance "drinks poison in her heart";[15] and the child who is taught the thrust and to strike with steel as soon as he has left his mother's arms is hardly likely to build a peaceful society. In the place of the old heroism of violence, the humanists try to substitute a new heroism of justice and peace.[16]

This aspect of the humanist protest reveals both their nearness to us and their distance from us. Our problem, too, is education; but it is not the education of princes.

NOTES

[1] Thomas Aquinas, *Summa Theologica*, II–II, q. 40.

[2] *Calendar and State Papers and MSS Relating to English Affairs, Existing in Venice*, ed. R. Brown, London (1867), p. 444; *Letters and Papers of the Reign of Henry VIII*, ed. Brewer, London (1862), vol. 3, no. 3093.

[3] Innocent Righieri, *Cento Giucho Liberali et d'Ingenio* (1551).

[4] An interesting account of sixteenth-century militarism is given in *Past and Present* (July 1962), in an article by John Hale.

[5] For a very fully documented account of humanist attitudes see R. P. Adams, *The Better Part of Valour*, Washington U.P. (1962).

[6] The theme of Utopia is discussed in Adams, ch. 8.

[7] Augustine, *City of God*, trans. and commented Vives, London (1620), p. 150, quoted by Adams, p. 193.

[8] Erasmus, *Against War*, ed. Mackail Boston (1901), p. 10; quoted by Adams, p. 10.

[9] Erasmus, *In Praise of Folly*; quoted by Adams, pp. 46–7.

[10] Erasmus, *The Soldier and the Carthusian*; quoted by Adams, pp. 216–17.

[11] Erasmus, *In Praise of Folly*, O.U.P. (1913), pp. 166–78.

[12] Erasmus, *Against War*, quoted by Adams, p. 245.

[13] Erasmus, *A Soldier's Life*, in *Familiar Colloquies*, trans. Bailey, London (1725), pp. 172–7.

[14] Vives, *Introduction to Wisdom*; quoted by Adams, p. 239.

[15] Vives, *Instruction of a Christian Woman*, trans. R. Hyrde London (1541).

[16] Erasmus, *Concerning the Aims and Methods of Education*, quoted by Adams, p. 297.

5. THE ACCOMMODATION IN A SYSTEM

WHILE the humanists protested in this way against the growth of violence, the theologians worked along different lines. In the sixteenth century, the "neo-scholastics" got down to the task of organizing and polishing up the just-war tradition which they had inherited remotely from St Augustine.

Their central thought, most clearly expressed by Thomas Aquinas in the thirteenth century,[1] was that war could be regarded as an instrument of justice in international life, and therefore as an important tool for the benefit of humanity, if used in the right way. The idea depends on a comparison between the internal life of a nation, in which the individuals are ruled by the State, with the life of the international "community", in which the states themselves are like individuals (though, regrettably, there is no world State). In the international community, as in the national one, there must be order. Internally, every state finds it necessary to have some system of justice, and to use some form of judicial punishment in order to restrain its criminals; clearly, someone must do the same job in the international community. But in the international community, there are "sovereigns"—that is, states or princes who are, by definition, supreme; and as they have no superiors, no-one could keep order if they did not do so. Therefore sovereigns must have a judicial right of punishment in international matters, just as they have in internal matters; the only alternative would be international chaos.

This idea gives positive status to war as an instrument of justice; and, in spite of all the careful restrictions as to its use, this is the central light which illuminates the whole system. Only in the light of this idea can we understand either the detail or the general arrangement of great neo-scholastic treatises, such as those of Vittoria and Suarez.

The main emphasis, first of all, is on the *conditions of the just war*—that is, on the reasons which would make the original decision to go to war a just decision. Because war is essentially an instrument of justice, obviously the quasi-judicial decision of the judge-State which first "tries" the case is of central importance.

These "conditions" are best understood under the three categories of St Thomas: legitimate authority, just cause, and right intention. There must be legitimate authority: that is, the war must be declared by a genuinely *sovereign* state, since this is the basis of the whole system, and only sovereigns have judicial capacity. There must be a *just cause*: that is, a crime must have been committed, a grave right violated, for which there is no other remedy than war (there is, of course, much discussion as to the details of these international crimes). Finally, there must be *right intention*: that means that the warring state must intend to promote the good and avoid the evil—and under this last condition we could group the notorious "rules of proportionality", which require the sovereign to weigh up the possible good results of the war against the possible evil results—and to decide whether victory itself is *probable enough* to justify such a dangerous means of achieving it.

The other subjects discussed are detailed problems arising out of the main theme.

There is, first of all, the very obvious problem of how one supreme being can punish another supreme being; but this is fairly easily solved by an intellectual manœuvre. According to the usual explanation, a state which commits an offence becomes, by that very act, subject to the state which it injures, in respect of that particular act; automatically, therefore, the injured state becomes both judge and executioner of the offending one.

As to the actual conduct of the war, the rules drawn up depend entirely on the judge-criminal relationship. Strictly speaking, there are no general "rules of warfare"; there are only rules for the conduct of war by the *just side*—the others have no right to be fighting at all, and their only duty would be to surrender! You could not expect the just-war thinkers to draw up rules about how a policeman could be assaulted, or how a judge should be assassinated! So far as the just side is concerned, it must not do unnecessary harm, but at the same time it must not neglect its function as judge and punisher. With regard to prisoners of war, Vittoria considers that it would not be "a violation of justice" if guilty prisoners were put to death;[2] and, with regard to the sacking of cities, Suarez considers that this is permissible if it is required by the gravity of the offence or by the need to deter other offenders.[3] When, and if, the just side is victorious, peace has been established and the wrong redressed, there is still the need to *punish*—because, if a state can do this to its own citizens, "society at large can do it to all wicked and dangerous folk, and this can only be done through the instrumentality of justice".[4]

It is important that war should be effective, if it is an instrument of justice; and a state will not be effective in war unless it is united. It is, as we shall see, an essential part of the logic of war to stress authority, obedience, conformity; the ideas are continuous from Augustine to Clausewitz. For the neo-scholastics, this conformity is necessary in the cause of justice, because war is in the cause of justice. The question of conformity comes to the fore when the rights and duties of individuals within the warring state are discussed —has the soldier, for instance, or the prominent citizen, any right or duty to enquire into the justice of his prince's wars? It is Suarez who is the most coherent, and who "perfects" the tradition on these points. His predecessors had been inclined to say that prominent citizens, at least, had a duty to enquire, because *charity* would require them to save their sovereigns from the great evil of fighting an unjust war, if they were in a position to do so. Suarez, however, saw that war just *would not work* if many people felt such obligations— and if it did not work there would be no point in having a just-war theory at all! The sovereign is the judge; the people must have an effective instrument, not a crowd of squabbling auxiliary judges. Charity, he argues, the sort of charity which might lead a man to interfere with his prince, only binds "in a case of necessity" (he does not elaborate this); much greater stress is to be placed on *obedience*. He does admit, grudgingly, that if a soldier has very grave positive doubts about his prince's wars—that is, if he is practically certain that they are unjust—then he has a duty to enquire; but as to what he should do after his enquiries, no guidance is given—the matter is left discreetly alone.[5]

Neutrality is another question which comes strongly under the influence of the central theme. There is no "right" of neutrality in the just-war tradition—this is a very modern idea. The reason is obvious, as soon as one realizes that war is being considered precisely as an instrument of order for the benefit of the whole international community. There can be no right of neutrality, any more than an individual can have a right to stand by impartially and watch a policeman being beaten up by a bandit. A country may perhaps be neutral because it cannot make up its mind who is right and who is wrong; but this unfortunate state of affairs should not continue—the "neutral" country should hurry up and find out who is on the right side, and then join in to help.[6]

It is obvious that the just-war theory sails very close to rocks which threaten at times to wreck the ship. The worst difficulty to get round is that the theory violates one of the best-established principles of human justice, that no-one should be the judge in his own cause. The principle is the most basic common sense, and is founded on the well established fact that people usually support their own causes, and therefore will always tend to judge themselves in the right! In the just-war pattern, each sovereign is called upon to constitute himself as judge of the "enemy" (which he cannot do without pre-judging that he has received an injury), and then to adjudicate in his own case and mete out his own punishments.

The difficulty is serious enough in theory, and perhaps insuperable in practice. The theorists manage to negotiate the rocks, and are well aware of their presence. This accounts for some further manœuvres and subtleties.

There is a good deal of discussion, for instance, about how certain a sovereign has to be of the justice of his cause, and whether he is bound to consult with wise men before he makes his decision. The general view is that he must consult, and that he must be absolutely certain; and in the course of the arguments for this point of view we occasionally catch a glimpse of the evident peril that is being circumnavigated— the peril that all sovereigns will always judge themselves right, and so there will be international chaos. Not only this, but there may be logical chaos too, which is worse. Vittoria thinks that if the sovereigns judge themselves to be right they *are right* because they are rightful judges, and therefore, if they were not very seriously restricted in their judging powers, many wars would be just on both sides—and that would mean that all the belligerents would be innocent and could not be killed!

Suarez is more ruthless and perhaps more logical in his philosophy of violence. He is primarily concerned that the instrument of war should work. Where his predecessors see chaos resulting from going to war on merely *probable* grounds, he sees chaos in waiting for certainty. Decisions, after all, must be made, and a just judge in a matter of distributive justice should favour the more probable view.[7] Suarez feels the same way about the degree of certainty of victory which is required to make a war just. To wait for absolute certainty, he thinks, would be quite impracticable— and in any case, while you were waiting for your moral certainty you might lose an important advantage! Probability of victory is therefore enough.[8] Extreme though these views are, they have a certain cogency; they are part of the logic of violence.

What is curious, at first sight, in all these arguments, is the lack of emphasis on the idea of arbitration, compulsory or otherwise, as a means of settling international disputes. The idea occasionally puts in an appearance, but a very hesitant one. Suarez, for instance, considers there is some obligation to go to arbitration only when two sovereigns, neither of whom is in possession, both have an equally probable claim to territory—and presumably they would first have to agree that their claims were equal! Even so, the idea of compulsory arbitration is hedged about with all kinds of safeguards for sovereignty.[9]

Others put forward a slightly stronger case for arbitration in some circumstances—but at some cost in logical consistency. For the difficulty of "judging the judges" is a logical one. If they are "sovereigns" they cannot be forced to do anything! And it is on the fact that there are such sovereigns that the whole just-war theory is based.

Sovereignty means no compulsory arbitration; and yet international order *may* mean compulsory arbitration. This is the difficulty which hovers in the background. Perhaps it is only the working out of a deep contradiction in the original notion—the notion of an ordered community of "sovereigns".

1. THE SCRIPTURES IN BRACKETS

St Augustine's thought about war, we may remember, was in a state of tension. On the one hand, he felt bound to concede, with the world, that it was possible to fight in war and yet to be a Christian; but on the other hand, he was always aware that the early Christian tradition, which was an important part of himself, and the teaching and example of Christ in the Scriptures, pulled in another direction. The tension could only be resolved by appealing to *Deus ex machina*, and the idea of a war begun by God's direct authority.

By the time of the neo-scholastics, however, the tensions were all resolved. There was no difficulty about the tradition of the Church, because pacifism was simply heresy—something "out there", to be condemned and rejected, and that was that. The early Christians had thought of themselves as an army of light drawn up against an army of darkness—and the army of darkness was the Roman Army with its legions. The neo-scholastics had the same impression of themselves as an army of light; but the army of darkness drawn up against them were the heretics—and among them, all the pacifists were to be found.

Deus ex machina, moreover, had come down to earth

in the form of the natural law. The natural law taught that whatever was written into the nature of man, or of society, and was there "read" by man's natural reason, was a natural revelation of God, the author of nature, and could be used to supplement the Scriptures. The theory is a good one, and should not be rashly discarded; but it is obviously open to abuse. In practice, the whole just-war theory which we have outlined, claimed to be the necessary conclusion of rational reflection about human society, and claimed, therefore, to be God's own just-war theory, part of the natural law.

There remained the difficulty of the Scriptures, which at first sight seem to have something to say against violence. But here a whole tradition of interpretation was there to help, and the war against heretics helped to discredit *a priori* any attempted pacifist exposition of Christ's teaching. What resulted was a systematic technique of diminishing the meaning of the Scriptures, and even a reversal of their original significance.

The technique is not applied maliciously, but is the inevitable result of looking for a certain type of religious systematization. We demand, as it were, a clear black-and-white pattern, in which every conceivable human act is either ticked or crossed by the heavenly schoolmaster; and we regard the Gospels as a sort of divine answer-book. We feel pressed, as St Augustine was, to "allow" violence in the present state of the world, in certain circumstances. Therefore, we must conclude, these violent acts must be white, and not black; therefore, if we thought the Gospels were saying something about the unholiness of violence in general, we must have been wrong. What we read could have had nothing to do with this sort of situation; on the contrary, if we read the Bible carefully enough, it must say that these acts are white and not black—for is it not the divine answer-book?

The result is a progressive tightening of a noose round the non-violent teaching of the Gospels, until the very life-blood often ceases to flow. The "neck" which is constricted is the Sermon on the Mount, and the whole story of the birth and the crucifixion of Christ, with the lesson to Peter which forms an integral part of it—"He who takes the sword shall perish by the sword." The rope from which the noose is made is fashioned from a number of "peripheral" texts— texts which are not really about violence at all, but which can be interpreted as implying an oblique kind of approval on the part of Christ for that kind of action which we wish to find "ticked".

Four typical techniques of constriction are to be found among the just-war theorists.

The first is to limit the application of the Gospels to "inward" acts. St Augustine set the ball rolling by accepting the obvious meaning of the precepts of patience, but saying that they were only binding in the innermost sanctuary of the heart. Certainly he, and St Thomas who followed him, stressed that the inward dispositions should always be seeking outward expression; but it is a fairly easy step from the "inward disposition" theory to saying that, as precepts, these teachings have *nothing to do with outward acts*; and this clears the decks for a "natural-law" theory of outward acts which has no need to take account of the troublesome texts.

Another constrictive device is to ask, not what is *commanded* by the Gospel, but what is *forbidden* by it. Of course, if the Gospel is a divine "answer-book", it comes to the same thing—to know what is wrong is the same thing as to know what is right (as long as a simple two-value system is assumed). We can, therefore, take the text, "Revenge not yourselves, my beloved" (which continues, "If your enemy is hungry, give him to eat") and ask, What is forbidden by this? The answer is clear: Revenge is forbidden. Therefore, so long as vengeance is avoided, we shall be "on the right side". We are free, now, to elaborate a just-war theory which is concerned (not with vengeance, of course!) but with just punishment.

A third constriction is to divide the teaching of Jesus into "precepts" and "counsels"—the first being necessary, and the second unnecessary. Then, if the difficult texts are accepted at their face value, they can still be regarded as only an "optional extra", to be undertaken by special people, but no part of the essential fabric of salvation. They are like the extra sums at the end of the exercise, to be done by the "good boys"; or like the decoration on the Christmas cake, not connected with the quality of the real cake inside. Again, the effect is to put the Scriptures in brackets so far as the natural-law scheme of justice is concerned.

Yet another constriction of great importance in the history of Christian ethics is to distinguish *public acts* from *private acts*, and to limit the application of certain teachings to the private sphere. The advice to Peter,

"He who takes the sword shall perish by the sword", was understood by the early Church to mean what it said—perhaps in a crudely literal sense. But from the fourth century onwards, it was taken to apply only to private acts of violence. If the executioner took the sword—or if the soldier took it as a public servant—then obviously this was quite outside the scope of Jesus's warning.

At the beginning of his great treatise on the just war, Suarez has to deal, very briefly, with the pacifist heresy. He considers, in turn, all the notorious "pacifist" texts, and dismisses them in turn by the various interpretative devices which are outlined here. His conclusion is that they are all irrelevant; and this enables him to carry on with his well-ordered and logical treatise without further reference to them. He has indeed dismissed pacifism; but Christians today are beginning to wonder whether he has thrown out the baby with the bathwater.

2. THE WORLD IN BRACKETS

It is easy to see how, by the necessity of their system, the just-war theorists were obliged to put the Scriptures in brackets; but they were equally obliged, and again by the necessity of the system, to put the world in brackets. The humanists had been mainly concerned with "war-as-it-was"—that is, with the whole sordid human reality of war, with the hatreds, murders, lust, and general moral degradation which they saw in its very texture. The just-war thinkers, on the other hand, were apparently concerned, not with "war-as-it-was"

but with "war-in-itself"; they were concerned to understand it, as a possible part of the rational structure of
a rational society, as an instrument of justice. From
their point of view, the sordid reality had certainly to
be taken into account, as one of the disadvantages a
prince should "weigh up" when he was deciding
whether to make war or not; but it was not part of
the essential structure, and was therefore not of very
great theoretical importance.

One problem connected with the sordid reality
threatened to break out of the brackets in which it was
confined; and this was the problem of the killing of
the innocent, which was so hard to fit into any coherent
moral pattern that it sometimes threatened to wreck
the whole system. It was therefore urgent to keep it
safely "within bounds", in the confines of private
ethics. The problem could, of course, easily be solved
in general terms, by arguing that the killing of innocent
people was no part of war-in-itself, and need not therefore be specially considered, any more than the question of rape, or the problem of war orphans. But the
killing of the innocent was in fact a difficulty of a
more pressing kind; partly because murder is contrary
both to the clearest law of God and to the deepest instincts of human nature, and partly because it was
recognized, even in the sixteenth century, as an almost
inevitable accompaniment of war-as-it-was.

It was at this point that the "double-effect" principle
had an important part to play in the development of the
just-war ethic; and, as this principle has now become
much more important than it was for the classical
theorists, it would be worth while to trace its origins.[10]

We all know that our actions have complicated results, some of which we approve, and some of which we
do not approve. A moral act is like throwing a stone
into a pool—the ripples spread out indefinitely, the
cross-currents become more and more complex, until
even the most acute mind would be baffled in the
attempt to plot them. All our actions in fact have
multiple effects; how then are we to act responsibly in
such a confusing situation? Most of the time there is
no problem at all. We live in what we have defined,
by a kind of personal moral intuition, as our own
centre of responsibility, and we discount, without
having to think about it, the results of our actions
which lie outside the limit. Only on odd occasions does
the problem of multiple consequences thrust itself upon
us, when we become aware of some particularly choppy
cross-currents in the obvious results of what we intend
to do. In such cases, we define the limits of our
responsibility in a rough and ready way, in such
phrases as: "I must do what is right, and I cannot
help it if x is offended", or, "That [bad result] is not
worth worrying about", or, "It's worth the risk."

In the sixteenth century, these commonsense judge-
ments were put into an apparently precise and logical
form by some Spanish theologians, and came to be
known as the rules of double effect—rules, that is,
which lay down the precise conditions on which we
can rightly do something in spite of the fact that we
foresee certain bad consequences. The commonest
formula is this: An act with two effects, one good, and
the other bad, is lawful, on four conditions. First, the
action, viewed in itself, must be good or at least in-

different; secondly, you must not intend the evil effect, but only the good; thirdly, the good effect must be produced as immediately as (that is, not by means of) the bad; and fourthly, there must be a sufficiently weighty reason for permitting the evil.

This sounds cumbersome and elaborate, but it is not unlike the common sense on which it was originally based; and this can fairly easily be seen if we consider the first examples with which the Spanish theologians worked. They were, on the whole, cases of "scruples"; and there are three or four stock cases which often re-appear: whether a classical student should go on read-ing the salacious Latin poet, Martial, even though he finds he is sexually aroused in the process; whether a girl should walk through the street, knowing she will arouse the passions of the local youth; whether a butcher should sell meat to a Jew, knowing it will be used for heretical practices. If anyone really had any difficulties over such decisions, he or she would be in a rather peculiar mental state; but it is conceivable that they could be helped to define their area of responsi-bility by the "rules of double effect", and carry on with their normal activities.

Once the rules were formulated, however, they were found to have "expandability"; they opened up almost endless vistas for the evasion of responsibility. In the seventeenth century, people could be found teaching that it was all right for a man to hold the ladder for his burglar-master, so long as he only intended to avoid getting the sack; or that a man might wish for and rejoice at his parents' death so long as he only had in mind the benefit to himself. In short, you could get away with almost anything, so long as you kept your "intention" on some good aspect of what was going on.[11]

All these false developments were condemned; but the expandability of the double-effect principles was inescapable. The rules were, after all, made up in the first place not to prevent things being done, but to *permit* them to be done; and the apparent safeguards against unreasonable expansion proved illusory. It seems a good, firm idea, to begin with, to say that the action must not be "bad in itself"; but this is really begging the question, because an act will not be bad-in-itself if it is "covered" by double-effect. The idea that you must not get your good result *through* the bad one seems a good safeguard, but it brings up all kinds of difficult problems about causality; and the rule about a "sufficiently weighty reason" would not be likely to prove much of a stumbling-block for anyone who wanted to do a bit of stretching of the rules.[12]

There remained the rule about not *intending* the evil—but this proved the most slippery of all. It was perhaps some kind of safeguard, as long as "intend" meant what most people meant by "intend", because the common sense of ordinary moral responsibility is built in to the ordinary use of the word. But an odd thing happened to this word "intend" in the double-effect tradition, when another stream of thought flowed in, which seems to have started with St Thomas Aquinas. For a long time, Augustine's teaching that you could not kill in self-defence had been at odds with the accepted moral practice of Christendom, which recognized that you could kill in self-defence without sin;

St Thomas tried to bring the two contradictories together by saying that you could kill an assailant so
long as you did not intend to kill him, but to defend
yourself; the killing was then "accidental". Now
obviously, when the problem is raised of whether you
can kill in self-defence, you are not concerned about
whether you can kill "accidentally", but whether you
can kill intentionally—that is, in the ordinary meaning
of the words "accident" and "intention"; there's not
much point in arguing about what kind of accidents
you are permitted to have. But St Thomas's ruling
gave the impression that there was some special, theological sense of "intention", through which you could
avoid responsibility, even though you "intended" to
do something wrong according to the ordinary, non-
theological use of words. Once this "double-effect
killing" joined the classical student and the modest
maiden and the scrupulous butcher as an instance of
"double-effect", the idea of "intention" in the rules
became uprooted from ordinary usage, and the last
safeguard against the "expandability" of the rules dis-
appeared.

So far as the just-war tradition was concerned, however, this was a gain; for it provided a splendid device
for circumnavigating the difficulty of "morally" killing
innocent people—and, incidentally, any difficulty arising from the evils that attend on warfare. All of these
can be regarded as "accidental"—"covered by the
double-effect". This is of course the same thing as
saying that they are not part of the *essential structure*
of war, with which the just-war tradition is concerned;
but it succeeds, in addition, in pushing the problem

4+

of murder right back out of the just-war field, where it threatened to cause havoc, and back into the sphere of personal ethics, where it was less dangerous; for, even if the killing of the innocent were seen as a necessary part of the war—even if, in the ordinary sense of the word, it was *intended*—it would still be possible to say that it was "accidental" in a special, theoretical sense. The just-war system then would remain intact.

The double-effect rule does not, as I have said, play such a large part in neo-scholastic thought as it does today; but the effect it has of abstracting the theoretical discussion altogether from urgent moral issues is typical of this way of thinking. The general result is an odd lack of apparent concern with history. To the belligerent Renaissance prince, the learned moral theologian, apparently representing the Christian tradition, propounds this solemn lesson: You must not go to war unless you have a fair chance of winning, and unless you are fairly sure you are in the right; to the subject, of whatever status, he says, "Do as you are told!" Another moralist observes sternly, wagging his finger at the "unjust" belligerent, "whoever has been justly and legitimately condemned may not defend himself against his legitimate judge!"

By setting aside the world and the Gospels, these theologians were able to achieve an unusual degree of clarity in their thinking about war as an instrument of justice, which gives them an interesting place in the prehistory of international law; indeed, some of their thinking may become much more relevant in the future, when there is a system of international justice, than it has been in the past. Since, however, their speculations were remote from revelation, they are not to be regarded as an important part of the Christian tradition—still less as an extra revelation; and, since they "put the world in brackets", it is hardly surprising that the world put them in brackets, and that they had, so far as we can judge, no influence on the course of political events.

NOTES

[1] Thomas Aquinas, *Summa Theologica*, II–II, q. 40.

[2] Quoted, *A Code of International Ethics*, Catholic Social Guild, Oxford (1937), p. 85.

[3] Suarez, *De Bello* (Section X of *De Legibus ac Deo Legislatore*), 16.

[4] Quoted by Eppstein, *The Catholic Tradition of the Law of Nations*, p. 102.

[5] Suarez, 4, 10.

[6] Y. de la Brière, *Le Droit de Juste Guerre*, Paris (1938), pp. 124ff.

[7] Suarez, 1, 3.

[8] Suarez, 4, 10.

[9] Suarez, 6, 4.

[10] For the history of the double effect see the article by G. Ghoos in *Ephemerides Theologicae Lovanienses*, vol. 27 (1951), pp. 30–52.

[11] Examples of double-effect excesses mentioned by E. Anscombe, *Nuclear Weapons and Christian Conscience* (ed. Walter Stein), London, Merlin Press (1962), p. 58.

[12] The rules are subjected to an interesting criticism by W. Macdonald, *Principles of Moral Science*, Dublin (1910), pp. 187–209.

6. THE CONSECRATION IN HISTORY

WHAT did matter to the world, however, was the crusading spirit, the institution of medieval chivalry, and the national militarism which eventually grew from it; for these historical movements rooted deep in human nature.[1]

1. THE MIDDLE AGES

War in the Middle Ages was primarily the business of princes and of knights, who held land in return for military service. "Bearing arms" was, like hunting, the privilege of the landed aristocracy, and it was largely through them that the tradition of chivalry was in the first place cultivated and passed on.

The privilege was a jealously guarded one. The Middle Ages had a strong sense of hierarchy, of the way of life appropriate to each caste. The knights fought, the clergy prayed, the people laboured; and those who transgressed outside their proper limits could meet with severe social disapproval. A French chronicler, writing after the Battle of Senlis, in 1418, recorded that "there was a captain who had a crowd of footmen, and they all died; and there was great laughter, because they were all men of low estate." A crowd of peasants who took arms for their emperor, Henry IV of Germany, in 1078, met with more savage punishment; they were castrated after the battle by the feudal lords for presuming to bear the arms of knighthood.[2] The punishment, apart from its savagery, was symbolic. The privilege of "bearing arms" has long been associated with the attainment of the full dignity of manhood, and it is appropriate that those who, being of low estate and not fully "men", presume to assume the status of knights, should in revenge be deprived of their manhood.

In the late Middle Ages, however, the tide of a new culture began to rise ominously round the islands of feudal privilege. The towns rose and prospered; and in the towns, fighting became more and more the business of hired men, "soldiers" (from *solidus*, a shilling) who were recruited by *condottieri*, hired for a particular job, and then dismissed, if possible, when the job was over.

It was the towns which provided this new economic pattern, the army developed, and it was the new floating urban population which provided the recruits; but they would fight anywhere—they had no particular regional loyalties. Switzerland was an international recruiting-ground, and Swiss mercenaries were to be found in all armies. They are still to be found, in name at least, in the precincts of the Vatican.

This development was taking place independently of the old feudal pattern, and began to undermine it. At the same time, the changing techniques of war were making the knight-in-armour increasingly anachronistic. England's victories against France in the Hundred Years' War, at Crecy, Poitiers and Agincourt, were mainly due to the fact that England had stolen a march on France in the arms race, by organizing trained companies of longbowmen, who toppled the loosely organized gangs of French knights off their horses, encased in their clumsy boxes of plate steel, before there could be any proper chivalric combat. The names of these battles have passed into the glorious myth of English history. But what is of much greater significance for European history is that they rang the knell of chivalry, at least in its old trappings. The knights were defeated by mercenary companies, the so-called "yeomen of England", using new techniques of mass assault. The French took a long time to learn the lesson, but it was a lesson that had to be learnt; the knights would have to go.

2. THE RENAISSANCE

The introduction of gunpowder, and the very rapid development of artillery in the sixteenth century, caused a further technical revolution in the methods of war, and at the same time the standing national armies took shape. The feudal armies had not been "standing" armies. They were professional fighters, but they had only come together for battles. The mercenary armies were originally disbanded as well at the end of wars, but this proved more and more difficult. It is not so easy to give a mass of people the sack, and the soldiers probably had no other trade. The problem became particularly acute at the end of the Hundred Years' War. In England, it is not a coincidence that an absurd and prolonged civil war broke out, the Wars of the Roses, only three years after the long struggle with France was over; the unemployed were not out of work for very long. In France, King Charles VII faced more seriously the difficult problem of disbanding his now superfluous men of war; and he eventually adopted the plan of choosing a select band of soldiers, and employing them to chase away the others after they had all been paid off. The only snag with this plan was that it left him with the select few; and in this way, by an odd irony of circumstance, the first standing national army was born.

The sixteenth century saw the establishment of national standing armies, and the suppression of local bands, in all the great nation states. Chivalry was now quite out of date; but this left a problem for the chivalric class. What were they to do to maintain the prestige, and even the employment, which was traditionally theirs? The new armies were taking away their work, and the rising bourgeoisie was challenging their privilege in many fields.

There was one major opportunity. The bourgeois did not, on the whole, want to take an active part in the new armies; they would finance them, but they would not serve in them. The nobility, on the other hand, had war in their blood, and they also had the tradition of authority. What more fitting than that they should take over the command of the growing military power of the nations? In general, this is what happened throughout Europe. In the centuries which followed, the nobility increasingly monopolized all the positions of command in the national forces, and they inevitably developed a strong vested interest in developing and increasing the military bureaucracy. In France, a military order of 1781 required a candidate for a sub-lieutenancy to show a pedigree of at least four noble ancestors. In Prussia, the *Junker* class always provided the majority of military officers, who formed a bureaucracy dangerously independent of the civil government. In England, the close involvement of the nobility in parliamentary government as well as in the army tended to dilute their militarism, but the same pattern can still be seen. The privilege of the nobility lingers on in the quaint notion of the "officer type" and in the prestige of the so-called "cavalry" regiments.

The "Junker" officers of the European armies helped to guarantee the continuity of European militarism. They brought with them from the Middle Ages the traditions of chivalry, the cult of the military virtues, and the notion of "honour", which they kept alive in peacetime through the class institution of the "duel" —a headache for governments until well into the nineteenth century. As well as this, they brought with them the exclusiveness of the old military caste, the sense of privilege linked with the cult of honour. Shakespeare's Henry V, according honour and nobility to all who fought with him upon St Crispin's Day, was probably more an ideal and a dream than a reality; the arrogance and overbearing class-consciousness of Coriolanus was probably nearer the reality, for all its remote setting.

3. TRICOLORE AND MARSEILLAISE: THE NINETEENTH-CENTURY EXPLOSION

During the French Revolution and the wars which followed it the old aristocratic militarism was forged into the new weapon of modern war in the fire of democracy and nationalism. The new self-awareness of the common people was born of a violent and massive attack on vested privilege and aristocracy; soon, however, the mass violence was outwards, under Napoleon, against the neighbouring states, and fused with an older militarism. In this way began a series of new-style international conflicts, of which we may not yet have seen the end.

Napoleon was not a revolutionary, but perhaps the most successful of all counter-revolutionaries in that he diverted the energies of the Revolution for his own ends. He was himself educated in the École militaire, the military academy founded in Paris for the sons of down-and-out noblemen, and he had many ties and sympathies with the old élite. By skilful manipulation of the masses, however, he was able to form a powerful alliance between their nationalism and democratic idealism, and the militarism and ambitions of the aristocracy. The famous *levée en masse*, which sought to bring the entire manpower and the whole resources of the French nation into the service of war, was not of course Napoleon's invention, but it helped to forge the tool with which he worked. The Légion d'honneur, which he did found, opened the magic treasury of "honour" to all ranks, military and civil, who merited it by their devotion to the cause of the Republic, and to the "fight for liberty and equality against all enterprises which tended to re-establish feudalism". "I ennoble all Frenchmen", he said. "Everyone can be proud." But at the same time, the old hierarchy was preserved. Of Napoleon's twenty-five marshals, nineteen had been in the army during the monarchy, and eight of these had been officers of noble birth. Many

4*

émigré officers returned from exile, of course, and Napoleon himself married into the house of Hapsburg.

Prussia, at once inspired and humiliated by the power of her aggressive neighbour, was obliged to respond to this new violence by seeking similar resources within the German nation. Small professional armies, schooled in old-fashioned tactics, were no match for the national and revolutionary enthusiasm of the French, and soon German military reformers were demanding that the latent resources of the nation should be liberated to meet the force of France. Give us a *national* army, was the plea. "What infinite resources there are slumbering within the womb of the nation, undeveloped and unused! Within the breast of thousands and thousands of people a great spirit lives whose upward-striving genius their low conditions paralyze."[3] The military reformers speak with an apparent revolutionary zeal; but their aim is only to awaken the greater potentialities of violence. "Only by bringing the mind of nations to excitement and fermentation," wrote one of them, "can they be brought to an unfolding of all their moral and physical powers."[4]

The Prussian Army, then, was vastly enlarged to include the *Landwehr* and the *Landsturm*, the old standing army, with its military elite, remaining supreme in authority and prestige. The Order of the Iron Cross was founded with the same touch of the democratic spirit as the Légion d'honneur. The development of militarism in Prussia mirrored that in France, though the old nobility remained more firmly in control.

From the revolutionary wars, the technique and the

cult of mass violence flowed out through Europe, and the image of war, transfigured and glorified by the poetic imagination, became an important constituent of the Romantic Movement. The Catholic philosopher, Joseph de Maistre, who lived through the Napoleonic Wars, wrote: "War is divine by the mysterious glory which surrounds it, and by the equally inexplicable attraction which draws us towards it; it is divine by the manner of its declaration; it is divine because it exalts and perfects nations."[5]

The Crusaders, never far below the surface of the European consciousness, once more emerged as a potent force, and the language of chivalry gained a new lease of life. The heroes of the ancient world were placed back on their lofty pedestals, and the military virtues were once more in the literary limelight. In England the folly of the Crimean War produced the even greater folly of Tennyson's *Charge of the Light Brigade*.

4. CLAUSEWITZ AND THE LOGIC OF VIOLENCE

More important than the work of the Romantics, however, was the lucid doctrine of the great Prussian military thinker, Von Clausewitz, who had been schooled in the campaigns against Napoleon. He taught in the Prussian military colleges, and his theories were subsequently accepted throughout Europe.

His thought is brutal in its simplicity, and yet it is cogent and strangely prophetic; for what he discerns is nothing other than the logic of violence itself, embodied in the actual historical situation, and his principle is to comply with this logic.

War, as he sees it, is the ultimate clash of force with force, in the elemental struggle between nations for existence or supremacy, which is the essence of international power politics. War is, in other words, simply the continuation of politics by "other means"; but these other means are also the ultimate means. The final measuring of force against force is like the cash settlement in trade; it may seldom actually take place, but nevertheless all transactions assume it, and are directed towards it.[6]

Since war is such an ultimate conflict, it follows that any principle of moderation is intrinsically absurd. As he puts it: "He who uses force unsparingly, without reference to the bloodshed involved, must obtain a superiority if his adversary uses less vigour in its application. The former then dictates the law to the latter, and both proceed to extremities, to which the only limitations are those imposed by the amount of counteracting force on each side ... to introduce into a philosophy of war a principle of moderation would be an absurdity. War is an act of violence pushed to its utmost bounds."[7]

Of course, Clausewitz explains that he is only talking about the essence of war, and says that each particular war will be conditioned and perhaps moderated by accidental circumstances. All the same, war in itself, as he conceives it—violence pushed to its utmost bounds—is set as an ideal, a directing point, for the war leader, the "original measure of all his hopes and fears", which he should approach whenever he is able or forced to do so. Prophetically, Clausewitz pronounces a law of increasing hostility: "The greater and deeper the antagonism between nations, the more war will approach to its absolute form."

Naturally, the war leader, who bears the responsibility for the ultimate conflict, is the supreme hero of mankind; and the pursuit of the military profession—Clausewitz's own—is the highest intellectual activity.

5. THE CANCEROUS GROWTH; TOTAL WAR IN THE TWENTIETH CENTURY

Clausewitz leads us to the threshhold of the twentieth century. He was adopted doctor of military matters by the French after their defeat in the Franco-Prussian War, and Marshal Foch used him as a textbook in the French Staff College in the years immediately preceding the 1914–18 War. Nor was his influence by any means confined to these two countries. A wartime English edition of Clausewitz's little digest, *The Principles of War*, published in 1943, quotes with approval from the German edition published seven years earlier: "Only if we understand the nature of warfare in the spirit of Clausewitz can we hope to maintain our existence in case necessity should once again force the sword into our hands."[8]

Clausewitz, like a true prophet, conspired with history.

The desire for total suppression of the enemy found its historical expression in the demand for unconditional surrender, and the corresponding rejection of a negotiated peace. The policy was broached by the allied generals in the First World War, and helped to draw it out to unnecessary lengths. It was adopted by Adolf Hitler in *Mein Kampf* as the inevitable principle of all future wars. "The great masses", he wrote, "will demand in the war to come the victory of the stronger, and the *annihilation or unconditional surrender* of the weaker." During the war, Roosevelt and Churchill made unconditional surrender the avowed policy of the Allies; and this policy led to a refusal to negotiate a peace with Japan before the crimes of Hiroshima and Nagasaki had demonstrated the "absolute supremacy" of the victors.

The policy of unconditional surrender is of course condemned by responsible moralists, since it makes victory more important than justice, or than human life; but we should not pass it by without noticing that there is a logic in the approach to Clausewitz's ideal. The greater one's commitment to violence, the greater the demand for total suppression, and it is hard to stop, either in theory or in practice, anywhere along this line. The total enmity of one side will always serve to "justify" the total enmity of the other; and you cannot negotiate with a total enemy, any more than you can make a truce with the devil. Only destruction and defeat make sense.

The demand for total suppression has been matched by the development of the techniques of total suppression; and the development of the techniques of total suppression is only part of the progress of science. The cancer of total war has grown inevitably with the material progress, and in a sense with the moral progress, of modern man.

The arms race itself is of course a very old problem. The Cobden-Bright group in the 1830s advocated arbitration and disarmament, because they saw no limit to the increase of arms—for "the progress of scientific knowledge will lead to a constant increase of expenditure." They were right, of course. There has, in a sense, been an arms race at least since the English jumped a step ahead of the French by using the long-bow in the Hundred Years' War. If nations are committed to, or even prepared for, the "ultimate resolution of conflicts" by violent means, it would be absurd to suggest that they should deprive themselves of the most effective means; if science starts to race, then armaments are certain to race with it.

The "saturation raids" developed by the Allies towards the end of the 1939–45 War marked an important stage in the developing technique of total destruction. On 3 August 1943 Hamburg, after enduring ten days of concentrated air raids, was so saturated with high explosives and incendiaries that 60,000 acres of the populous centre of Hamburg "took fire", and were consumed in what came to be known as a "firestorm".[9] This does not just mean that all the buildings were separately burning, as may have been the case in some streets in London three years before. It means, rather, that the whole city began to function as one huge furnace. It means, therefore, that those who had taken refuge in deep shelters were gradually roasted alive as the temperature steadily rose; it means that some who tried to escape were carried into the centre of the furnace by the hot winds; and that people running in the streets suddenly became incandescent as the long flames licked towards them.

The effect at Hamburg was, in a way, accidental; but once the discovery had been made, it was later repeated deliberately—as, for instance, at Dresden, a non-military city, crowded with refugees, which was made into an "example".

The importance of Hamburg and Dresden is that they were mildly prophetic of things to come. There is no need to elaborate on the effects of the weapons we now possess. Most people know now that the old-fashioned atomic bombs were of a completely different order from anything used earlier in the War, and that they were mere pinpricks in comparison with the present thermonuclear missiles. There is no doubt that an important feature of any future large-scale war would be fire-storms of a kind we can only guess at.

The growth in the techniques of destruction and the moral demand for total suppression of the enemy have meant that the civilian population has become increasingly a direct object of attack. In the First World War, there were the odd Zeppelin raids, the sinking of the *Lusitania*, the bombing of Karlsruhe; in the Second World War the massive air raids, and the logical culmination in the total destruction of the cities of Hiroshima and Nagasaki. The future might hold even stranger developments, since it is probable that the strictly military targets will become increasingly invulnerable and impossible to locate—so that non-military targets will be the *exclusive* objects of attack! The only safe place to be will be in a Polaris submarine—the only legitimate military target!

Most moralists condemn the direct attack on civilians, since it is hard to deny that this is murder, and most people are prepared to agree that murder is wrong. There are undeniably innocent people in "enemy" cities—women and children, the sick and the aged—and if killing them is not murder, what is? There are, however, other voices among the "moralists"; there are those who talk about *indirect* killing, which is not "intended", and then enlarge this convenient category to cover any action they wish to justify; and there are others, perhaps more honest, who say that the enemy nation *as a whole* is "guilty", and therefore to be attacked. Here is the logic of violence, and we should not underestimate its force. In the Second World War, the *total attack* on populations was matched by a *total commitment* of populations; nations were moulded together as never before in a fervour of democratic and nationalistic idealism. The whole economy and industry of nations were geared to war, and through the complexity of the modern economic structure nearly everyone was involved in "war-work". Conscription only by-passed those able-bodied men engaged on work of "national importance". Even those digging their gardens were "digging for victory", on both sides. Whole nations cohered as never before about one great hero-figure, and this hero, in each case, not a military but a civilian leader; yet no-one would have thought of talking about "Roosevelt's wars" in America, or about "Churchill's wars" in England, or about "Hitler's wars" in Germany, as they may once have thought about "Henry VIII's wars". These were wars of total commitment; and, although Christian theology may know nothing of any kind of "collective guilt" which would justify acts of genocide, total commitment and total violence do go hand in hand—they are just different aspects of the general advance towards Clausewitz's absolute. There is an element of inconsistency, even an element of folly, in introducing a principle of moderation; and this is the real force underlying "moral" arguments for acts which seem, in another perspective, the extreme of barbarism.

This total commitment is itself part of the total force of a country. Nothing succeeds like the will to win. The French Revolution revealed the overwhelming force of passionately held beliefs; and the Clausewitzian military theorists of the nineteenth century stressed the will to win to such an extent that the arms race actually slowed down—there was too much stress on numbers and morale, and too little on technique, and this was partly responsible for the enormous losses in France in the 1914–18 War. The arms race soon got under way again through the stimulus of conflict, but the battle of minds did not diminish. The "moral" problem, so far as the military were concerned, became simply the "morale" problem. Propaganda designed to boost one's own side, or undermine the other, to build up the impression that the struggle is life-and-death conflict between absolute good and absolute evil, becomes increasingly more important, more *part of the war*; it is directed by civilians, and its growth is inseparable from the development of mass media of communication. The growth of war and the growth of modern society have gone hand in hand.

Last of all, the cancer extends in time. For total commitment to total violence cannot be achieved in a moment, either morally or materially; consequently, the enemy of the future must be faced now—faced by the economy of a country, by its industrial organization, and faced also by a total commitment on the part of the Government and the people—because such commitment is itself a part of the force, and the force must be total. There must be no break in the will to enmity, no break in the alliance. The ultimate logic of violence, in fact, is to destroy the enemy here and now, without waiting for him to destroy you first. This is the policy of the pre-emptive strike, once seriously discussed on both sides of the Iron Curtain.

It is often said that there is nothing radically new about the problem of war today; and, although this needs a lot of qualification, it is true in one very important respect. Limited wars were a product of civilization, always liable to erupt, through the inner stress of violence, into outbursts of total destruction. What has made its reappearance on the stage of the twentieth century is the barbaric phenomenon of total war, the normal pattern of primitive group enmity.

What is unique about the present situation is that, partly through culpable negligence and partly through sheer lack of understanding, we have allowed the primitive pattern of total enmity to grow to its full natural dimensions and to become incorporated in the very fabric of a complex civilization developing in a way increasingly beyond our control. The result of this is that we are now faced with massive structural problems which cannot be solved simply in terms of their origins.

NOTES

[1] Alfred Vagts, *History of Militarism*, New York, Meridian Books (1959), p. 42.
[2] Quoted by Vagts, p. 42.

[3] Quoted by Vagts, p. 131.

[4] Quoted by Vagts, p. 132.

[5] Joseph de Maistre, *Soirées de Saint-Pétersbourg* (7th. con-versation).

[6] Quoted with approval by Engels; see Marx and Engels, *Gesamtausgabe*, series 3, ch. 2, pp. 270ff.

[7] Quoted by Vagts, p. 182.

[8] Clausewitz, *The Principles of War*, London (1942).

[9] The bombing of Hamburg is described by Martin Caidin in *The Night Hamburg Died*, New York, Ballantyne Books (1960).

PART 3

7. WORLD UNITY AND THE BALANCE OF POWER

I F violence tends always towards complete destruction of the enemy, it tends also to provoke a corresponding violent response. We have seen how the development of militarism in Europe since the Napoleonic Wars was in a symmetrical pattern, as countries with largely the same cultural backgrounds and technical capabilities were provoked in turn to copy each other's violent initiatives.

1. THE BALANCE OF TERROR

The outstanding feature of the present situation is that violence has apparently reached its ultimate development both in its destructiveness and in its symmetry. The countries which, in different ways, share the inheritance of Christendom, have polarized into two power blocs, which both possess the power, and perhaps the will, to destroy each other in an incredibly short space of time.[1]

Yet they have not done so. There is little reason to doubt that this is partly because of the symmetry between them—because of the notorious "balance of terror". Each side has, or will soon have, a virtually invulnerable second-strike capacity—that means, each is capable, even if devastated by a nuclear attack, of launching an equally devastating counter-attack. The Americans achieve this invulnerability by burying their

"Minuteman" missiles in hardened sites which can be destroyed only by a direct hit and by loading nuclear weapons on to Polaris submarines, which move around the oceans continuously so that their position will never be accurately known by an enemy. The Russians achieve their invulnerability mainly by keeping their rocket sites secret—a kind of invulnerability which is, unfortunately, very vulnerable to spying. The result of this is that both sides have a credible second-strike capacity, and neither could use its weapons without facing almost certain destruction.

The balance, though it may seem effective, is neither safe nor stable. New delivery systems are being devised, and new defence systems; any major breakthrough by either side could upset the balance of deterrence, and could increase the risk of war. Consequently, both sides feel obliged to spend fantastic sums on armaments and weapon research.

Those who see the absurdity of the position, and those who sincerely desire peace, see no way out of the balance of power dilemma which will not increase the danger of an already dangerous situation.

2. ANOTHER WAY: THE UN

It has often been argued that the UN really makes precious little difference to these facts of power politics, and to the balance of violence which has just been described.

The attack on the "Monster of Turtle Bay",[2] as the organization has been called, is easy—in theory, at least. Its initiatives are ruled by the Security Council; and in the Security Council the great powers face each other, just as they do in the world outside. The Council can do nothing unless all its members agree; and it seems absurd to think that they could ever agree about the major conflict. Consequently, it looks as if the UN could only deal effectively with side-issues; and in any case, the Charter itself permits "regional defensive organizations" to take action on their own behalf—and as both sides can obviously regard themselves as regional defensive organizations, one might think the Cold War would remain quite untouched by interference.

Underlying these arguments, there is a deeper criticism which seems unanswerable; and that is that the UN, after all, has no *power*. There is a mockery of a military commission attached to the Security Council, but it has never functioned and is never likely to. The Monster has neither claws nor teeth; what could such a flabby beast do against the tigers of East and West? Not even the most civilized state can work unless it has power over its subjects; and how could the UN be expected to work in the international field while the power remains in the hands of the rival power groups?

In spite of all this, after eighteen years the UN is still with us; and, in a curious way, it seems to have acquired a great deal of prestige and even of *power*— though it has no nuclear weapons. It is beginning to show signs of being a vital organism, by which humanity is trying to adapt itself to a new challenge; and, like a living thing, it has grown, often in a way that was not foreseen by its parents, and yet in a way that makes sense.

The most striking aspect of this growth has been

the rise in the authority of the Secretary-General. In the original Charter, his powers were only very slightly defined—he had the power to report to the Security Council a threat to the peace; but that was about all. From this seed, however, a lot of shoots have grown. Trygve Lie, Hammarskjøld and U Thant have steadily enhanced the prestige and enlarged the scope of the Secretary-General's initiatives. If the Secretary has a right to report to the Security Council, he must also have a right to know the truth; and that means that he must not rely on any nation's propaganda, but must send personal representatives to trouble spots—or even go himself, as Hammarskjøld went to Laos in 1959. From these beginnings, UN "presences" have been established in various parts of the world, and have acquired a significance out of all proportion to their size; for through them, it is felt, unbiased information is fed back by expert observers to Turtle Bay, where it may influence the attitudes of over a hundred different nations.

Observation soon led to action. Because, unlike the Security Council, the Secretary-General was capable of acting, and was the person who could most be trusted to act impartially, Hammarskjøld first of all was entrusted on several occasions with independent peace-making missions, culminating in the climax and perhaps the tragedy of his career, the Congo operation. What is extraordinary about the UN operation in the Congo is that the Secretary-General was able to pursue on behalf of the UN a live and independent policy, nominally with the backing of the Security Council, and yet without the real support of the great nuclear powers. Britain probably opposed the operation throughout; and, when the US stood behind Kasavubu, and Russian clamoured for Gizenga, Hammarskjøld would have neither. What emerged from the chaos was the broadest-based government possible, which is still in power, though its success is problematical.

How is it that Hammarskjøld's initiatives were supported, and not vetoed, by any of the great powers? The answer is that there has been a shift of power downwards as well as upwards from the Security Council; downwards to the General Assembly, where each nation except China is represented by one vote. At the time of the Korean War, the General Assembly had passed a "Uniting for Peace" resolution, which enabled the Assembly itself to take action in a crisis if the Security Council was paralysed by the veto. The resolution had already been used to overwhelm the protests of Britain and France, when the Assembly asked the Secretary-General to organize a peace force to deal with the Suez crisis. The procedure could have been used again during the Congo affair; but in fact none of the Security Council wanted to be overruled by an overwhelming majority in the Assembly, as Britain had been at the time of Suez—they could achieve nothing but unpopularity by that. So the veto was not used.

What is striking about this power-shift in the UN is that it is a shift of power, paradoxically, *away from* the "powerful" antagonists; a shift upwards into the hands of the Secretary-General, who is necessarily impartial and from a small non-aligned nation—otherwise he would not be elected; and a shift downwards to the hundred-odd nations of the Assembly, many of them small and weak, and an ever-increasing number of them "uncommitted", voting according to the circumstances of the case, and rarely according to a Communist-anti-Communist line-up. More and more the "powerful" are having to listen to the "powerless".

But, it might be argued, there is an obvious limit to this development. Congo was a complex issue, and did not very closely involve the great powers. What about the Cuban crisis of 1962? Here supreme violence faced supreme violence; here was the reality of the world situation behind the superficial appearance—and what could the world organization do in such a crisis but hold its breath like the rest of us?

If we agree about these facts, we may well disagree as to whether this is the deepest *lesson* of the Cuban episode. What, for instance, did the Homeric giants actually achieve by their clash in the Caribbean? The US would claim that it had "defended the Western Hemisphere", the USSR that it had secured Cuba against invasion. Of the two claims, Krushchev's makes the most sense; for it was far more probable that the US intended to invade Cuba than that Krushchev intended to attack the Western Hemisphere. All the same, Krushchev did have to elicit a lot of very insubstantial promises from Kennedy in order to make it appear that the encounter had produced any positive results at all. For in fact the net material loss and gain was nil; the situation in the Caribbean remains what it was. If there was any gain at all, it was a gain for the whole world which has come to a more lively understanding of the true power situation; and that is, that massive violence has reached the stage of *complete sterility*—that the balance of force against force could really lead to the destruction of our civilization, or it could mercifully lead to a prolonged stalemate, but that it is quite incapable of solving any problems of order or of justice, and that it is becoming increasingly incapable even of producing any significant change in minor disputes.

We are, in fact, confronted with a massive stalemate of violence and enmity, which has spawned in many parts of the world to produce lesser stalemates which reflect the greater one. In Korea, in Berlin, in Indo-China, there have been limited conflicts, and no doubt their limitation is due in part to the nuclear deterrent —both sides, aware of the risks of unlimited conflict, tacitly agree to "rules of the game" which prevent its spread. But if these conflicts are limited because they are overshadowed by the massive conflict, they are, for the same reason, utterly sterile. The armistice commission still meets in Korea, South Vietnam remains a perpetual headache to the USA, and the Berlin problem seems perennial. There are of course special difficulties in every case; but there is a pattern which is becoming increasingly familiar. When local problems are approached *in terms of the Cold War*, the net result is, from the point of view of order and justice, a washout; the stalemate remains as stale as ever.

Problems press for solutions; and, when the voice of violence fails, it may well be that the voice of justice has a chance to make itself heard; perhaps this is the fundamental reason for the gradually emerging authority of the UN.

It may well be objected that it would be rash to
identify the voice of the UN with the voice of justice
—and so it would. But at the same time, it cannot be
denied that it is much more like the voice of justice
than anything we have yet heard on the international
stage; and this can easily be appreciated by comparing
it with its rivals.

The old just-war theories always came up against
two major obstacles. One was that for sovereign states
to judge their own causes was such a profound and
obvious violation of natural justice that it was hard to
build any sensible system on such a foundation; and
the other was to do with the essential opposition of
violence and justice—that it is extremely difficult to
make a system of justice out of international war without being involved at some point in the essential rule of
trial by battle, that might is right.

The initiatives of the UN avoid these snags. The
very basis of its authority is its impartiality; the shift
of power upwards to the Secretary-General and downwards to the Assembly is a move away from the Cold
War, away from preconceived alignments on disputed
issues. The choice of personnel shows an obvious concern for impartiality, so that justice is *seen* to be done
in this respect at least. In the Congo the UN was
represented in turn by an American negro and Nobel
Prizewinner, an Indian diplomat, an Irishman, and
an Australian. The Secretary-General's post itself has
been filled by two Swedes, and then by a Burmese,
whose impeccable career in the struggle of his own
country for independence makes him a very difficult

object for the slander of being a "tool of the imperial-
ists"—or, for that matter, of anyone else.

The second difficulty, that of basing a system of
justice on the capacity for violence, is also quite
evidently avoided by the UN, since whatever power
it has clearly is not based on the capacity for violence;
its emergence, on the contrary, has depended precisely
on the failure of violence to cope with the problem
of order. Its natural alignment is therefore with the
weak rather than with the strong; Hammarskjøld used
to say that his job was to take care of the small nations,
because the big ones could look after themselves.

Naturally, the small states and the newly emerging
"third world" look increasingly towards the UN as
their natural champion, and as the parliament where
they can at least make their voices heard. In spite of
all manner of pressures, the third-world nations,
whether they go Left or Right, show themselves disconcertingly independent of the great power blocs,
especially when their concern for justice is subordinated
to their concern for their own power. They gravitate
away from the centres of ineffective violence and towards the only possible centre of justice. This is one
of the more hopeful signs of the present international
structure.

3. WORLD ORDER: GRASS-ROOTS

While these developments are going on at the top,
the beginnings of a world order are taking shape in
international organizations, and, lower down, in a
less definite but no less real way, a sense of human

unity is beginning to take shape in the minds of men.

This growth of unity is a cultural movement so vast and complex, and one in which we are so intimately involved, that we shall have to wait for the historian of the twenty-first century to put it into perspective. At present, we can only indicate a few straws in the wind.

An important focus which helps to form men's minds to unity is present-day science—the same science which has magnified the problem of human enmity into the inescapable problem of nuclear war. In the physical and the biological sciences we seem to be on the threshold of new realms of thought of immeasurable significance for the human race as a whole; and all over the world, scientists, like the scholars of medieval Europe, speak in the same conceptual language, and use, when they can afford it, the same techniques. Knowledge flows rapidly and freely round the world, and significant progress is becoming more and more evidently the outcome of an intricate and worldwide co-operation of minds.

Exploration of outer space, of the upper atmosphere, large-scale investigations of the earth's geological structure, and investigation of the deep interior, all require scientists to work in a "laboratory" common to the whole of humanity, and all require worldwide co-ordination of effort. In addition, the very expenses involved are providing an ever-strengthening argument for the closest international co-ordination, and rivalry or duplication of effort in many fields is becoming not only absurd, but impossible.

It is not only scientists who are involved in science; we are all involved. As one of the focal points of our culture, science and the objects of scientific research have an imaginative significance which extends throughout society. While circling satellites and space-exploration make us increasingly aware of the earth as a unit, the home of man, so in the minute field of molecular biology, research into the infinitesimal structures by which organisms grow and propagate themselves, and into the essential nature of growth and decay, bring us close to central issues concerning the nature of man which go deeper than any divisions of race, creed or colour.

The development of communications, itself an important feature of our scientific culture, gives us a sense of belonging to the world just as vivid as the medieval Englishman's sense of belonging to England, though our world patriotism lags a little behind. If China had invaded India in the thirteenth century, we might have heard rumours and legends about it a generation afterwards. When China invaded India in the 1960s, the next morning we all felt immediately concerned, just as we should have been if there had been a riot in our own town—and with good reason, for international proximity is such that this now *is* our own town. When the Americans set out to elect their president, the world holds its breath, and some of us feel, not unreasonably, that we ought to have a vote. Wherever we travel, to the once "mysterious" East, the heart of "darkest" Africa, to the "frozen wastes" of the North, we shall probably find intelligent people reading newspapers or listening to the wireless, and

5+

discussing the same events—though from rather different points of view.

The unity that is emerging is, however, more than a material one; it also has its spiritual dimensions. Pope John, in his encyclical *Peace on Earth*, mentioned three distinctive features of the present age. One was the rise in the status of the working classes, another the rise in the status of women, and another the emancipation of subject races. Beneath all these movements, there is a general assertion of human dignity and responsibility, regardless of sex, status, religion, race —or even age, if we are to take the American child as a sign of things to come! Human rights are the battle-cry of the day; a Universal Convention of Human Rights is attached to the UN Charter, and Pope John's encyclical took the form in part of a human rights manifesto. The spiritual lava which erupted in the French Revolution has spread out over the whole surface of the earth. That is why *Peace on Earth* was received with such universal acclamation— though anti-Communists found it hard to see why Communists liked it, just as Communists found it hard to see why anti-Communists liked it. In their group organizations, people are everywhere stumbling towards new degrees of political and social awareness and responsibility; and, although the immediate result is division rather than unity, there is no doubt that the spiritual vitality which underlies these movements could be one of the binding forces of the emergent world community.

And yet there remains, we are told, the great schism. Two irreconcilable political and social systems face each other, determined to blast each other out of existence rather than to come to any form of doctrinal compromise. On the one hand, a creed of public ownership and control of all the means of production, on the other, free enterprise and ownership and control by private individuals. On the one hand, a one-party state, governing according to an "orthodox" historico-social doctrine, in the name of the proletariat, and calling this "democracy"; on the other hand, free criticism, and a party-system with two sides playing a spectacular kind of football game every few years to decide who will govern next, and calling this "democracy".

The opposition seems irreducible. And yet, as the two systems evolve and their problems change, the terms of the opposition become much less clear in practice than they are in theory. The harassed Russian "manager" is not so very different as we might have thought from the harassed Western executive—and neither is at all like either the typical "capitalist" or the typical "revolutionary". Free enterprise creeps into the East almost as persistently as public ownership creeps into the West. The one party becomes less monolithic, and the football teams find that they have to agree about most major issues in order to make any sense at all out of social progress. If they have their communal holidays, we have our Butlin's. Pope John spreads alarm in one camp by observing that "socialization" is a characteristic of our age, and the monster of "revisionism" occupies the attention of the big-game-hunting theorists of the Marxist camp. Meanwhile, in semi-secrecy, sociologists and economists begin to talk a slightly different language, neither capitalist nor Marxist, thinking of problems as problems, and solutions as solutions, in the context of the common challenge which faces both societies, and indeed the whole world: the staggering growth and complexity of industrial civilization.[3]

There *are* real conflicts, and precious values are involved; to stand aloof from such conflicts would not be sane. But to regard the present opposition between Communism and anti-Communism as an ultimate barrier to the unity of mankind would be to show a pitiful lack of historical perspective. Catholics and Protestants once thought that Christianity could only survive if they wiped their opponents off the map. Fortunately, neither of them succeeded, and eventually, a new virtue called "tolerance" emerged. Perhaps in the political field we shall be quicker to accept the brute fact that, however uncomfortable it feels, we have to share the world with a rival football team; and who knows what new political virtues could be born of such a realization?

The world has its possibilities. But, as a dim world-loyalty begins to illuminate the human situation, it reveals two massive problems in the field of justice. On the one hand, there is an appalling and still-increasing gap between the rich and the poor, between the millions who overeat and the millions who starve to death; and, on the other hand, there is the problem of how to organize justice in an international community which has always solved its problems by having duels, now that this system has become, to say the least of it, inappropriate.

This is the situation which faces Christians, as it faces everyone else. Which attitudes seem appropriate, and which inappropriate, if we are to be loyal both to our Christian heritage, and to the world? These are the questions I should like to consider in the following chapters.

NOTES

[1] A good account of the present deterrent policies is given by Strachey, *On the Prevention of War*, London, Macmillan (1962).

[2] The phrase is taken from Andrew Boyd, *United Nations; Piety, Myth and Truth*.

[3] For an account of the similarity-in-opposition of East and West see Raymond Aron, *Paix et Guerre*, Paris (1962), pp. 327ff.

8. INAPPROPRIATE ATTITUDES

1. PROTEST WITHOUT RESPONSIBILITY: THE GOSPELS WITHOUT THE WORLD

ALTHOUGH the teaching and example of Christ call us continuously away from violence and hatred and bloodshed, the world has a built-in resistance to this call. The tensions which result can be agonizing; and it is tempting to get rid of them straight away by various intellectual manœuvres. We can, for instance, pretend that the world does not exist, or that we are not responsible for it; or we can pretend that the Gospels do not apply to it. If these manœuvres are successful, then is the time to beware; for the tension between the world and the Gospels can only be removed by eliminating one of them; and both are necessary for a Christian in the world.

Of the three historic Christian attitudes which we have been considering, there can be no doubt that Protest is the most authentic in the light of the primitive tradition. The early Christians thought of themselves as building a new spiritual kingdom with the sword of the spirit, and the Roman armies were little more than a diabolical parody of the real power which flowed from Calvary; it is for us to recapture, in a twentieth-century way, the vitality of their vision.

Jesus' rejection of violence cannot be ignored. It was a rejection rooted in history, and it had profound historical consequences. The Jews were a proud and a conquered race, smarting with resentment against their Roman overlords, and longing for the day when they should be once more a powerful and independent nation. The "Zealots" were always for armed revolt, and, a little before the birth of Jesus, a rebellion had been put down savagely by the Roman authorities. No doubt, when the Jews looked forward to the coming of the Messiah, they hoped for a great military leader. In rejecting violence Jesus shattered their hopes, but founded a religion which eventually conquered the conquerors, and remained to form a new civilization when the Roman Empire crumbled to pieces.

Throughout the centuries, the theme of non-violence has been held on to by various sects, usually labelled "heretical", and by monks. The most interesting and influential of recent groups has been the Society of Friends, or Quakers. This group had its origin in the midst of the bloodthirsty wars of religion in seventeenth-century England, when Cromwell and his Puritans were intent on building a new Jerusalem in England by force of arms. As this exploit degenerated, rather like the Crusades, into a senseless orgy, the Quakers emerged to affirm their twin principles—that the Kingdom of God is within every man, and that it is not promoted by violence. Like that of the early Christians, their non-violence was a kind of reaction-formation within a violent political situation; and it is not surprising that their first theologian, Robert Barclay, linked their beliefs with those of the early Fathers, and so established a tradition to which they have remained extraordinarily faithful.

As total violence grew to its full dimensions in the

two world wars, Quakers have become more and more clearly aware that the great enemy of man is hatred itself. When war was declared, they declared war on hatred; and by their courageous and impartial service in the Friends' Ambulance Unit, they earned the respect of all, and had an influence out of all proportion to their numbers.

The Friends, on the whole, stand for a total protest against violence, and therefore against all policies based on force or the threat of force in any form. They are joined in their general protests against modern war and all warlike preparations by various other groups of more "limited" pacifists: by philosophers in the humanist tradition, who dwell on the utter absurdity of modern war, and on the threatened extinction of the human race; and by Christians of all denominations, who hold that, whatever the situation in the past, war now clearly involves the deliberate killing of innocent people, which is plain murder, and therefore must be utterly and unconditionally rejected, since it involves violation of a commandment which all accept as bed-rock. Even the threat of war, as in a deterrence policy, is sometimes said to imply an intention to murder in certain circumstances, and therefore to be already mortally sinful.[1]

What could be more relevant, one might ask, than such protests, at a time when statesmen and generals seem to contemplate the burning of cities full of people with the same equanimity with which Catholics and Protestants once set about destroying each other one by one on public squares? Indeed, the protest is relevant; none of these positions just outlined is to be lightly brushed aside. Every Christian must have a protester in his heart; anyone who has not learned to weep over the savagery and hatred of modern war can hardly claim to have made any contact with the mind of Christ. The horror that the Christian feels is not that of being killed, but that of killing; not that of being a martyr, but of being a murderer; not the fear of suffering with Christ, but that of crucifying him afresh in the person of our fellow men. This is the backbone of our tradition, and must be the backbone of an informed Christian conscience.

Yet, in spite of this, there are some natural accompaniments of the attitude of protest which seem inappropriate to the modern condition of man.

One of the characteristics of the present day is a kind of political coming-of-age; an increased awareness of political and social responsibility, and, corresponding to this, an increased scope for political and social action which can affect the structure of the society in which we live. We are not in the same position as the early Christians, who fostered a new religion in the bosom of tyrannical Rome, or as the Renaissance humanists, who ultimately could do little but obey their princes, and try to educate better ones for the next generation. For a Christian of our times to avoid the issue of intelligent political commitment could be a heavy failure of responsibility at a time when responsibility is most urgently demanded; it might, in fact, be nothing but a continuation of that "apartheid" of Christianity from politics which has much to do with our present difficulties, and this could well make the situation worse rather than better.

5*

In the face of the violence-ridden world, there are three possible courses of action. Either we can renounce it as hopelessly corrupt; or we can try to change it abruptly, saying that there is no hope for the monster unless it completely changes its heart, or its spots, or both; or else we can accept it as it is, with all its complexity of good and evil, seek out its growing points, its potentialities, and then strive with the utmost vigour, and yet with the utmost patience, to foster this growth, to realize these potentialities, and to co-operate with the Holy Spirit in bringing good out of evil.

The first two attitudes are common attitudes of protest, and apparently enable us to be loyal to the Scriptures or to our ideals with little sense of intellectual strain or difficulty. The world is evil; cast it off, tell it about its wickedness, and you have separated yourself from its guilt and stood up for the truth. The third attitude is harder, more tortuous, and full of agonizing compromise; for, once it is accepted that the world cannot be changed here-and-now, and that we are nevertheless still responsible members of it, we shall become involved in the evil of it. There may come a breaking point where this strain becomes intolerable, and where the only course for the Christian is an ultimate refusal; but, in the meantime, it is only in the third way that we can act responsibly in the political dimension of our lives.

There is something else in the attitude of non-committed protest which is profoundly disquieting. To "reject" the world, or to try to change it abruptly, from "the outside", according to a preconceived pattern, is to suggest that there is a division between the world and the rejector; that there is, as it were, a community of grace, detached from the community of the graceless, and that one can cross over from one camp to the other and shake the dust from one's feet. Part of our Christian tradition seems to say this. And yet there is a growing feeling, as the human race converges, a feeling hard to define but deeply significant, that we are all, the whole of humanity, *in the same boat*—and that to move from one part of the boat to another does not make such a difference, even morally, as people used to think. There are moral difficulties in which we are communally involved, and from which we cannot so easily detach ourselves by acts of the intellect and of the will. What is called for rather is good temper and good navigation.

The community of the graceful and the community of the graceless seem to have become hopelessly mixed up. It is not only that the dust sticks to our feet when we change camps, but that grace itself seems increasingly hard to confine. No sooner do we say it is just "here", or "there", than it puts in an appearance somewhere else. From "graceless" heresy comes new wisdom, from "graceless" industrialism a moral advance in family life, from "graceless" social science a charity more delicate than any we are likely to hear of from the pulpit. While pious Christians, glutted with "supernatural" virtues, gloat over their boxing-matches, it is the brain-surgeons and not their pastors who observe that, though their virtues may be supernatural, their entertainment is subhuman.

The world remains with us, though we reject it; and

grace remains in the world, though we fail to see it. Nowadays, the Holy Spirit seems to have become disconcertingly catholic.

The field of international relations, nuclear deterrence, power politics, tedious conferences and ponderous supranational institutions seems to be an unpromising field for his activity; but at least we should wait and see.

2. ACCOMMODATION IN THE SKY:
NEITHER THE WORLD NOR THE GOSPELS

Some kind of "accommodation" to the world seems to be required if Christians are not just to remain aloof from international policies and the emerging world order.

St Augustine first tried to make such an accommodation, and the scholastics later wrote up this accommodation into a systematic theory. Today, this theory still has its protagonists among professional moralists, and in the inarticulate form it is the usual means of adjustment adopted by those who feel there is a moral difficulty about war. How are we to regard this accommodation in its present form and in the present situation?

Broadly speaking, the problem of the just war is still debated in its traditional form. The central emphasis is on the three conditions which make an original decision to go to war a "just" one; namely, sovereign authority, just cause, and right intention. The just-war protagonists insist that these three conditions can still be fulfilled, and that there is still, therefore, a real possibility of a "just war". Consequently, we have no right to go round "objecting" to war, but must be realistic, make adequate preparations, and fight if necessary, though working at the same time for peace. These moralists are opposed by a small but growing group who admit that the just-war conditions make sense in theory, but that they are not fulfilled in practice in modern war, that they are morally certain not to be fulfilled in any large-scale future war, and that therefore we must simply "object", and refuse to countenance any preparations for such a war, or to take any part in it.

All the conditions of the just-war theory provide material for this debate. First, war must be declared by a "sovereign"; but are nation-states still sovereign in the relevant sense of the word? The anti-war group is inclined to say that they are not; there is an international court, there is the United Nations, there is, at least in embryo, an international police force—does it make any sense in these circumstances to say that sovereignty should in justice still be attributed to nation states? It does make sense, reply the just-war protagonists; until there is a much more adequate world order, there must still be national sovereignty. Secondly, there must be a just cause; but can there be any just cause, when the evil involved by war would seem so heavily to outweigh any good to be achieved? The anti-war group would say there can be no such cause. The just-war protagonists would agree that the possible "just causes" were now very restricted in view of the degree of violence involved, but would insist that in the case of direct aggression by the enemy, each state must still have its inalienable right of self-defence; then, and perhaps then only, the evils risked by war would be outweighed by the importance of "self-preservation", or "preservation of the values of civilization". Sometimes, "necessity" is thrown into the balance along with these to make sure the scales tip the right way.

The peripheral problems, those relating to the conduct of war rather than the conditions founding the just war, come in for fuller and rather more humane treatment than they were accorded by the sixteenth-century moralists; but they are still treated in the spirit of the original theory. As war is essentially an act of international justice against an international criminal, it makes no sense to talk about "rules of war" applying to both sides, for the wrong side has no right to be fighting at all. It makes no sense, either, to talk about the "right" of neutrality, for it is a duty for all to join in on the right side; and conscientious objection is similarly out of favour.

The difficulty concerning murder comes in for special consideration. The anti-war group see murder as a necessary part of modern war, and cannot see how murder can be just. The "double-effect" theory, however, is capable of almost unlimited expansion, and now plays an important part in just-war theory. It is a sort of spiritual third-party insurance, readily available at the small expense of a little common sense.

I have no intention here of going into the intricacies of the just-war debate. I wish instead to step back a little from the debate, and to consider why the whole approach of the just-war theorists seems to be an extremely inappropriate one for a responsible Christian to adopt in the present situation.

In the first place, it involves today, as it always did, a rejection of the Christian tradition of non-violence and of the obvious meaning of Scripture on this subject. All the old devices of "constriction", traditionally used to narrow down the scope of Christ's teaching, are still applied with extraordinary clumsiness by just-war theorists, who have, out of the necessity of the system, to prove that the apparently "pacifist" texts are quite irrelevant. They are "counsels", not "commandments"; they apply to inner, not outward acts; you can love the person, and hate the sin; they apply to private acts, not to public acts, and so on. Every appearance of a soldier in the Gospels is hailed as a scriptural proof of the just-war theory, and the command of Jesus to Peter to "put up his sword" is contrasted with his earlier instruction to "go and buy a sword". All this must be infinitely regrettable to a sensitive Christian today, when sound Scripture scholarship is becoming a source of new life and unity in the Church, and when it is more and more evident that to leave it behind and embark on a new path is, after all, to leave behind the revealed Word of God. Moreover, this treatment of the Gospels is a great source of scandal to those who, like Gandhi, can see for themselves what the Scriptures are about.

When Jesus was asked, "Who is my neighbour?", his answer was enshrined in the parable of the Good Samaritan; if we were to put it in a logical form, that answer would seem to be, "It's up to you who your neighbour is." We can imagine that, if he had been asked, "What sphere of human activity does your teaching apply to?", his answer would have been along similar lines.

At least, it may be objected, the just-war theory enables us to think realistically about the world, and to play a responsible part in it. Though it is sad that it puts the Scriptures in brackets, should we not at least keep it for its relevance to international conflict? Unfortunately, the just-war theory is in many ways just as poor a tool for shaping international order as it is for the interpretation of Scripture. Indeed, it is not designed to be a "tool" in this sense at all—it is not in itself a programme of action, it is not meant to "shape" anything; it is rather the absolute-truth-about-things, the abstract-justice-of-things—it is God's answer-book, according to which he ticks or crosses our actions; well worth knowing about, of course, if God really worked like that.

It is one thing to *comprehend* a situation in this abstract kind of way, and it is quite another to try and *regulate* it. The contrast is marked in the question of war. For, since about the middle of the nineteenth century, a tradition of international law and custom has gradually been developing of which the whole purpose is to regulate war, and effectively to reduce its scope. What is extraordinary about this tradition is that, in many ways, it has a completely different orientation from that of the just-war theory.

One of the original inspirations of the international-law tradition was the work of Henri Dunant, a Genevan who had seen the suffering of wounded soldiers on the battlefield who were deprived of medical care. He began, in the 1850s, a campaign to remedy this situation as far as possible by international regulation. His efforts were eventually crowned with success by the signing of the first International Convention at Geneva concerning the care of wounded soldiers, from this beginning there rapidly grew up the movement we know as the International Red Cross—its motto *Inter Arma Caritas*.

In accord with this original inspiration, a central concern of international regulations has always been subjects like the treatment of prisoners, the treatment of wounded, the treatment of non-combatants, the conduct of neutral states—all those problems, in fact, which were peripheral for the just-war theorists; problems which they touched on very lightly, if at all. What is more, there was never the slightest question of rules applying to one side, and not to the other; there was only the question of rules which everyone would be prepared to accept, both on the grounds of common humanity and of mutual self-interest, to reduce the area of violence.

The sharpest contrast in the manner of treating these subjects was in the question of neutrality. Instead of being a regrettable situation in which some nations find themselves for lack of information, neutrality in international law now becomes a proper status, carefully safeguarded by every possible rule. Neutrals have international privileges of inviolability, and must observe a strict code of conduct in return for these privileges. The neutral has some of the status in international law that the just belligerent has in the just-war theory;

while the just belligerent, as a subject for special regulation, simply ceases to exist.

The reason for this is quite evident. There is no special treatment of the "just belligerent" in international law, because there is virtually no discussion of the conditions of the just war, the pseudo-legal rules by which a sovereign state, judging its own cause, can sanction its own wars and then use its own armies as an international police force. This does not mean that the problem of the actual initiation of war has not at all occupied the minds of international lawyers, treaty-makers, and convention writers; on the contrary, this has been their perpetual concern. The consistent direction of all their endeavours, however, has been to establish means for the independent and peaceful arbitration of disputes, to persuade nations to renounce the use of international violence, in short to *outlaw war*.

Of course, the communal effort of mankind to outlaw war at the level of international institutions has not yet succeeded, even in theory. The UN Charter, the latest stage of development, and the custom of nations, clearly reserve the right of individual and collective self-defence. What is the difference, one might ask, between the theory of the just war now and the international law? There seems to be little, in the abstract. Yet a comparison of recent studies in international law with works of some enthusiastic "just-war" protagonists reveals a different orientation of thought. "Self-defence" as a possible plea of defence for a nation charged with the crime of war before an international court of justice is a very different matter from self-defence asserted as an inalienable right of the sovereign state, a diminished survival of a much more general right of war, in the just-war theory. There is a similar difference between saying that self-defence is a possible defence in a murder trial, and saying that everyone, in general, has a right to kill other people, but that nowadays you should only do so if you consider it necessary. It is almost as if, in the first case, we see a tide of justice rising round small islands of violence; and, in the other, we sometimes have a vision of just-war enthusiasts dancing on the islands shouting, "We can still fight here, boys!"

The fact is that the two traditions in some ways start from diametrically opposed viewpoints. The just-war theory, for all its restriction, remains essentially a theory, as its name suggests, of the *justice of war*, and the sovereignty of nations; whereas international law, from the very necessity of effectiveness, starts from an implicit assumption of the *injustice of war*, and the interdependence of nations. Thus in international law violence can be little more than a temporary breakdown of justice, a breakdown to be prevented if possible, and if not, limited in its scope, like a forest fire.

To talk in the abstract about "rights of self-defence", "necessity", "self-preservation", outside the perspective of third-party judgement and established law, is unfortunately to say nothing in any way relevant to the situation. These are nothing but the stock formulas by which nations have always justified their actions,[2] though they are now becoming unfashionable. They are doctrines which are dangerously vague and elastic, liable to confuse rather than to clarify. However much they are hedged about by resounding protests against "aggressive wars", wars of "self-aggrandisement", and the "lust for conquest", the net effect of the proclamation of such doctrines is to leave people thinking and acting exactly as they thought and acted before.

The contrast can be illustrated in this way. There is not a single nation which would not readily agree with the latest formulations of the "just-war" theory, provided it remained as "abstract" as its authors intend it to be. We might say that the whole human race is completely agreed about the "conditions of the just war", and each nation would be quite happy to defend itself to itself on the pleas of "self-preservation", "self-defence", and "necessity". But once try to get a nation to agree to some small measure of international arbitration, to sign away the smallest part of its right to violence, to allow somebody else to judge what is and what is not "self-defence", and progress will be much more sticky. It is this progress which the world is struggling to make. It is depressing work; but the one consolation it has is that its very difficulty is a sign of progress. Just-war theory can be accepted without pangs; but only through the pangs of nations can international order come into being.

A certain South African bishop stated recently that there was "nothing in the Church's teaching to exclude the possibility of one state governing two races and maintaining their distinct identity". As a statement of principle, and a statement of fact, this seems unexceptionable. As a move in the world's struggle for human rights, and in the context of South Africa, it was questionable. It might have been better to say nothing.

Perhaps that was also Pope John's point, when he passed over the just-war tradition with discreet silence in his encyclical *Peace on Earth*.

3. THE BASIC DIFFICULTIES

What are the basic reasons for the contrary development of the just-war theory and international law? It is that two radical difficulties stand in the way of any idea of international order based on state sovereignty and the just war. These difficulties are difficulties of theory as well as of practice—they are there for those who try to "comprehend", as well as for those who try to "regulate". But whereas in *theory* it seemed possible to sail round these difficulties, in practice it is quite impossible to do so.

These two difficulties are, first of all, the problem of working a legal system in which everyone is the judge in his own cause; and also the contradictions which you come up against if you base "rights" on "violence".

The first difficulty was real enough for the Renaissance theorists, though it does not crop up much in modern discussions. Suarez admitted that there was something badly wrong with international justice as long as every sovereign had to judge his own cause, and even looked forward vaguely to a time when this would no longer be the case. In the meantime, however, he was quite content to elaborate a complex theory of justice in which nations do judge their own causes, since, as he argued, some form of justice is better than no form of justice. The difficulty, after all, was not a *radical* one; there *was* an objective right and wrong, there was justice-in-the-abstract, and, though it might be hard to get at it when you judged your own cause, it was obviously not impossible to do so.

International law could not in practice follow this path. For, if two opposing states, both sovereign, confronted each other in war, and each judged its own cause by an *authorized legal process*, the result was not at all hard to predict. Each would judge itself to be right, and, *legally speaking, each would be right*—because each was competent to judge. Consequently, if anything like the central "just-war" thesis were written into the international law, all wars would be just for both sides—which is of course nonsense both in practice and in theory. No wonder little attempt is made to build on such unsure foundations.

The intimate linking of violence with justice raises another kind of problem. It comes out in the just-war theory when there is discussion about how sure of victory you have to be before you go to war. Obviously, if war is a serious attempt to make things better, and not worse, you have to be reasonably sure of victory; otherwise you have no *right* to go to war. Equally obvious is it that stronger nations can normally be much more sure of victory than weaker ones, and their right of war is therefore much more extensive. Suarez is fully aware of this difficulty; if victory had to be certain, he observes, a weak nation would never be able to vindicate its rights against a stronger one—so he alters course a little at this point in his treatise.

He says you only have to be *fairly* sure (more than 50 per cent sure) of victory. Unfortunately, this still means that a *very* weak nation will have no right to resist the injustice of a very strong one—which, if anything, outrages our sense of justice even more.

For international law, the difficulty is radical, though it is a difficulty which is implicitly accepted rather than openly acknowledged. To accept in any sense a judgement by violence is to dig a grave for justice; if such a rule were to be written explicitly into the positive law of nations it would open up a prospect for the legal conquest of the whole world by one self-judging sovereign, whose supreme might would then be supremely right.

4. THE CONSECRATION OF WAR: THE WORLD WITHOUT THE GOSPELS

These radical difficulties in the just-war tradition, the difficulty of the self-judging sovereign and the difficulty of the calculation of victory, are both effectively obscured in the present situation by the liberal use of terms like "self-preservation", "self-defence" and "necessity". When we hear these words, the difficulty of judging our own cause seems to evaporate; we imagine someone flying at us with a knife, and there is no puzzle about our right to stop him, if we can; moreover, there seems to be need to enter into any calculations about the probability of success. When "necessity" is added to the stew, then clearly all questions of responsibility are resolved as if by magic.

In fact this is an appalling misrepresentation of the

real dilemma which faces mankind. The difficulty of the self-judging sovereign, and the difficulty of the probability of success, have now in reality grown to such dimensions that they can only be ignored by a moral lunatic; they have grown in exact proportion to the growth of total war.

If a major conflict were to take place between the two great power blocs, it would not in its origin bear much relationship to the crude simplicity of the "knife-attack". Krushchev is not going to say, out of the blue, "I'm going to kill you with my missiles, and what are you going to do about it?" If we want to know what might happen, we have only to think of the trouble spots which could most easily generate a major war. Cuba, South Vietnam, Berlin, perhaps Cyprus. Now, in every one of these cases very complex legal and moral issues are involved. We have President Kennedy's own testimony to the appalling injustice of America's past treatment of the Cuban people; many of us would have had reasonable doubts about dying for President Diem; and the London-Zürich agreement, which represents the British contribution to the Cyprus issue, is at least of questionable validity in the light of the UN Charter.

What we must face up to is the moral and legal complexity of these issues, the intensity of the passions which are involved, and, for those very reasons, the increasing absurdity of pretending that there can be a "just" and obvious resolution of these issues in terms of "right" and "wrong" so long as each side judges its own case. This strikes at the very basis of the "just-war" structure, which depends on first establishing the legality of the cause.

The difficulty of the calculation of success is just as formidable. Again, if one thinks in terms of a major clash between the power blocs, it seems obvious that such destruction would be involved that there could be no issue which could reasonably be solved in this way by either side. If we fought, the world would certainly be in such a mess that it would have been better not to fight; consequently, one might expect the just-war tradition simply to wind up at this point.

In spite of all this, some of its protagonists seem to be little oppressed by these difficulties. Why is this?

An easy answer would be that the "just-war" theory lived only in a realm of abstraction, where the ground of reality is lost below the cloud of hypotheses, and where any problem can be solved by a suitable manipulation of ideas. This is part of the truth; but it is by no means the most important part of it. The fact is that something like just-war thinking is a very vital force indeed, and in the minds of ordinary folk as well as in the manuals of moral philosophy. That it is right to fight when "necessary" for "self-defence" and "self-preservation", and that this, broadly speaking, "justifies" present policies, is indeed the most common attitude to the world situation.

So the problem remains. If the just-war tradition is a real expression of a real attitude to present international conflict, how does it, *in practice*, if not in theory, solve the real and agonizing difficulties which we have uncovered?

The fact is that the "bird's-eye view" in moral

matters is usually an illusion. The bird seems to be detached; but he must have taken off somewhere, and he is going to land somewhere; what is more, the "view" he takes from the air depends very much on where he has taken off, and what he intends to do when he lands. A moral bird's-eye view is normally built into a life of real moral commitment and direct moral perception of concrete situations, and, if this is recognized, the "view" can be a useful help in making choices; but, if this is not recognized, the upward flight can be morally dangerous. Either it will become a trivial game with no serious relationship to the world; or it will serve to conceal a moral choice which has already been made.

Throughout its long history, the just-war tradition has been much more incarnate than at first appears; much more bound to the actual historical situation than one would suspect from its lofty tone. St Augustine was concerned with the barbarian attack on imperial Rome; Vittoria with the Spanish colonization of Central America; Suarez with the wars against the heretical English. The just-war theorists of our day have one issue predominantly in mind; the clash between Communism and Capitalism.

"Purple patches" reveal the areas of emotional intensity. Most works of moral theology which touch on this problem of war, and yet remain at ease with the confines of the just-war tradition, are written for the most part in a "cool" style—straighforward, logical, colourless, rationally persuasive. At times, however, the language lights up with an unaccustomed glow. This is when Communism is discussed. Here a new rhetoric emerges, and a new vocabulary—"ruthless, tyrannical, atheistic, murderous, unscrupulous". These purple passages answer the first part of our puzzle.

The real problem of how, in justice, we can judge our own causes in international matters, is effectively solved by such writers, by a very simple but profound commitment. They have in mind only one major conflict; and *this conflict they have already prejudiced*, both in its generality and in its detail. They are certain, as if by the light of a supernatural revelation, who will be right and who will be wrong in every case; so, evidently, there is no puzzle about how to decide.

What of the second difficulty, that concerning the marriage of "right" to violence? Must we not say that a war, even of "self-defence", is unjust if it is just too damaging to all concerned? Again, the difficulty seems, in some way, to be effectively answered; and, again, the purple passages provide a clue. First, there are other places where the cool language of casuistry begins to glow. War, we are told, can be just, even if we are not going to "win" it because of "a higher obligation, that of respecting one's *plighted word*, of defending the higher values of civilization, of choosing *an heroic defeat* instead of an *inglorious capitulation*. The nations which have been *martyrs to their duty* render a supreme testimony to the right which *echoes through the centuries* and keeps humanity faithful to the *cult of honour and justice*".[3]

There is no mistaking this language, or its ancestry. Here the old heroic battle imagery floats up to the surface, here the voices of Mars and Wotan "echo through the centuries", here our crusading blood stirs in our hearts, and here, without any doubt, is the effective answer to the difficulty of how you can justly fight if you are not going to "win". If we were to put the answer in a logical form, it would be something like this: It is *always* right to fight for the right, because, even if you are defeated and killed, your heroic death in battle will further the cause of justice and bring you "glory". It is by a kind of act of faith in battle, and by a "light from above", that the difficulty is resolved.

Evidently, the words "sacrifice" and "martyr" acquire a new meaning in this context. The idea of a "martyr" who dies, not laying down his own life, but doing his best to lay down someone else's, would have seemed odd to the first generations of Christians. The new faith, however, is not compatible with the old. We can only prove that the violent response is always right because it is in a mysterious sense always effective, and "echoes through the centuries", if at the same time we take it as proved that no other kind of response to violence is ever effective, or "echoes through the centuries" in the same way. A position, needless to say, hard to reconcile with Christianity or with history.

It is appropriate to make fun of the creed of battle-heroism; but it would be folly to underestimate its force, or to demolish it without putting a stronger faith in its place. Language of this kind still taps a powerful source of psychological energy, and just-war language, through its very "neutrality" to violence, often succumbs to the magnetism. There is a dangerous slope downwards from the necessary war to the holy war, from accommodation to consecration; permitted violence becomes a right, then a duty, then a sacred duty, and we are right back where we started. The only way to cross this slope in safety is to hang firmly on to the Gospels.

The literature of our civilization from the earliest times is filled with the heroism in battle. The Crusades gave this theme once more an honoured place in the centre of our culture. We only have to go back to the generation of Chesterton and Belloc to find the perennial vitality of the crusading myth; but it is not just something which survives in literary circles. For all our apparent easy-going materialism, the majority of us are still warriors at heart, or in fantasy; almost any crowd can soon be aroused by an orator or a propagandist who can evoke from the depths the archetypal images of the fight to the death against the arch-foe in human form.

This is indeed the world without the Gospels. The least appropriate, and yet the commonest attitude of Christians in the present world crisis.

NOTES

[1] The best discussion of the question of murder is in the symposium edited by Walter Stein, *Nuclear Weapons and Christian Conscience*, London, Merlin Press (1962).

[2] See Ian Brownlie, *International Law and the Use of Force by States*, O.U.P. (1962), p. 48.

[3] *Code of International Ethics*, Oxford, Catholic Social Guild, p. 78; quoted with approval by MacReavy, *Peace and War*, Oxford, Catholic Social Guild (1963).

9. APPROPRIATE ATTITUDES

1. The Authentic Protest: Gospel against Hate

ONE sometimes has the impression that our understanding of Christianity is lopsided. Everyone seems to know that the words, "God is Love" somehow express what is most powerful and most original in the religion which flows from Calvary; and yet, if one asks what Christianity is against, the answers are bewildering in their variety. Some might say it was against sex, or swearing; some that it was against avarice, or alcohol; others, echoing a long tradition, that it was against pride. Few would say that it was against *hatred*; and yet, if love is the chief good, one might have thought enmity would be the chief harm —at least this would make for greater symmetry.

The lopsidedness is typical of real attitudes, as well as of theory. Few Church dignitaries, for instance, would openly use vile language—society would hardly allow them to; and they are well aware of the old enemy, the demon of impurity; but no-one would be outraged, or even surprised, to hear such professed Christians expressing violent antipathies—that is, hatreds—towards certain persons or classes or nations—or even towards one another. There is a demon here they do not take into account.

The Gospels do not show the same lack of symmetry. "Whoever shall say to his brother, Thou fool," said Jesus, "shall be in danger of hell-fire." Apart from this, there are only two occasions, outside the Parables, when "hell" is mentioned by Jesus as a punishment for specific sins; once, for those who fail to feed him when he is hungry, or to give him drink when he is thirsty; and on the other occasion for those who do harm to little children. The moments of greatest stress in the New Testament are the moments when the love of God washes up against the breakwaters of hard human hearts.

The same theme is common in the Epistles. James, for instance, wonders how it is that a man can bless God and curse his fellows with one and the same tongue; for it is unheard-of that the same spring should send out sweet and bitter water.[1] John observes that the man who hates his brother is a murderer[2]—a startling preview of Freud; and Peter only mentions the "conventional" vices to conclude that "charity covers a multitude of sins";[3] but this leaves nothing to "cover" hatred, which is the negation of charity itself, and poisons the very heart of a man.

To be concerned about hatred is to be concerned about violence; for violence, that is, action which has in view the damage or destruction of the object of violence, is the normal and natural incarnation of hatred. Of course, the link between violence and hatred is not "necessary" or "logical"—we can even *imagine* violence to a person being an expression of love, as with the heavy father who says, "This hurts me more than it hurts you!" But for all that, the connection is a very real one; even the "justest" retaliation or punishment is likely to have something akin to a momentary hatred about it, a momentary assertion of self and negation of the object. The association of violence with hatred is too intimate to be just "unthought".

Violence and hatred are normal; they are intimately bound up with the instinct of self-preservation, and that is why arguments which reach down to these roots are always powerful. Two responses make immediate sense when an animal is attacked—one is counter-attack, and the other is flight; both responses are often found in one situation—the cat which goes through its repertoire of violence for the benefit of an aggressive dog will disappear up a tree like a rifle-bullet if it gets half a chance. In human beings, the two reactions are prolonged and intensified by the passions of hatred, corresponding to counter-attack, and fear, corresponding to flight; the two passions are intimately connected, like the two primitive reactions which underlie them. The "violent" punisher—be he emperor or school-master—often fears for his safety, his authority, his prestige. Fear in the case of human beings only temporarily breaks the chain of violence, for it is always ready to change into hatred. Gandhi expressed this well, when he said to a Mussulman chief who was in revolt against the English, "Do not be afraid. He who fears, hates; he who hates, kills. You will break your sword, and throw it away; and fear will no longer touch you. I have been freed both from fear and from desire, so that I know the power of God."[4]

Violence grows by a chain-reaction, tending always to increase in intensity. The violent response has an inherent tendency to excess—not to balance, but to overwhelm the harm done—a scalp for a tooth, and two eyes for one eye. Even the Apostles suggested that they should send down fire from heaven to burn up a city which did not make him welcome, long before the time of nuclear bombs! But Jesus told them, "You do not know of what spirit you are."[5]

Sometimes the violent response may be submerged, but this does not necessarily mean that it is extinct. The natural response of a child who is hit is to hit back. If it happens to be an adult who has hit him, he knows that such a response is likely to provoke "overwhelming violence"; so he probably does not do it. But he may do one of two other things: he may "take it out" on someone else, or he may take it out *on himself*. It is well known that violent parents can be internalized as violent "super-egos"; and this may lead to a perpetual state of internal tension, to a strained and tense personality, which, in spite of superficial idealism, is highly unstable, and liable to explode into external violence at any moment. This of course is only one example of how violence can be perpetuated in a hidden way. What is true of children can be true, in different ways, of criminals, of nations, of racial groups. The recent ghastly revenge of the Watutsi in Ruanda against their former Hutu overlords is typical of the immemorial pattern of human behaviour.

It is obvious that the pattern of violent-stimulus-violent-response can always be justified at the rational level in terms of "retribution" and "self-defence". The violent stimulus at once provokes, "necessitates", and "deserves" a violent response; and, since men always have a powerful drive towards self-justification, these concepts can only too easily become a mere intellectual superstructure for a primitive hate-hate situation, and

6+

in themselves are very unlikely to point any way out of the vicious circle. That is why the progress of civilization has depended on establishing effective restriction and social control of these ideas in a way which prevents them from serving as the tools of passion.

Into this human situation the Christian revelation inserts as a central doctrine that we must *love our enemies*. This is nothing else than a direct frontal attack on "what comes naturally", a challenge to do violence to violence, and thereby to transform the primitive situation. Where the old law regulated violence, the new is creative, and makes enormous demands on spiritual resource and initiative. The command is not just to fight a defensive operation, but to attack the devil in his own murky territories, and build in them the fortress of love. This is the way in which we are to cut through the chain which links violence to violence, and to break out of the vicious circle of spiralling antagonisms.

But how on earth is it to be done? Confronted with this extraordinary paradox, Western tradition has often either rationalized it away altogether, or confined it safely to the region of the "supernatural". By a kind of secret grace-life in the centre of the soul, you "love" your enemies and your God in a completely supernatural, invisible, mystical kind of way, provided that you nourish this life by performing appropriate sacramental ceremonies. If Christians think this is the answer, they have little grounds for complaint if the world concludes that this kind of virtue is so completely supernatural that it is quite beyond having any relevance to real situations, and that the religion which maintains it should be left, like alchemy, to die a natural death.

What Christians surely have to realize is that the question, *How* to love one's enemies, is a serious and an intelligent one; and in trying to answer it, they may find that their faith suggests certain lines of thought and action which are very relevant to the challenge which faces our generation.

One sensible approach is suggested in the works of some modern French theologians.[6] To love one's enemy is to cultivate "le goût de l'ennemi"—to learn to hate with him the injustice which he rightly hates, and to love with him the justice which he rightly loves; an uncomfortable process, perhaps, because it could involve a sifting of one's own errors and prejudices from a "hostile" viewpoint. This could be a preliminary to a further effort in the way of intelligent love of enemies—to reduce the area of conflict, and progressively to extend the area of co-operation and peaceful debate. Beyond this again, there is the possibility of revealing to the "enemy" the hidden potentialities of justice in his own position—of "going another two miles" with the man who asks us to go one. Above, the concern of an intelligent enemy-lover is "not to resist evil"; that is, not to take up the "anti-position". How different would the course of history have been if the Church had taken more notice of this teaching!

"Depth psychology" could perhaps add another dimension to our understanding of this effort. The "enemy" is not just outside; he is inside too. He is the dark side of our personalities, which we may have crushed, ignored, neglected. There is internal violence here, which may become external when "the shadow" crosses our path in the form of another. How violent people often are in rebuking and condemning in others the faults which are deepest in themselves! Reconciliation with the enemy could be a means of healing—that is, of "holiness"—for the individual as well as for society. Perhaps that is why it is made the condition of adoption as "the children of the Father who is in heaven".[7]

Nothing could be a greater mistake, however, than to imagine that the love of enemies is simply a question of intellectual adjustment; since the violent response is built in to the whole personality, even down to the reflexes, the education which seeks to reverse this must be an education of the whole personality, of the emotions, instincts and reflexes as well as of the will. It is precisely at this level that the teaching of Jesus makes its first impact—if someone slaps you on the cheek, turn the other. "Absurd", we are inclined to think, "not to be taken literally"—and of course, it is not; but on the other hand, if the teaching is theorized away into an abstract "intellectual" activity, or into a mysterious supernaturalism, it loses all its vitality. It points to a whole educational programme; and in this Western Christianity has much to learn from the East, as well as from our own neglected humanist tradition.

Ahimsa[8] in Hindu thought was defined by Gandhi as, "A refusal of all harmful attitudes, even in thought, and even more of harmful actions, in regard to any creature, wherever such refusal can morally be exercized." Training for *ahimsa* is systematic, and involves overcoming a number of "preliminary obstacles". In these obstacles, the Christian is likely to see the old vices in a new light. Anger, which is nothing else than the momentary passion of hatred, comes back into focus as a central "obstacle", and can no longer be obscured by the pseudo-Christian idea of "righteous anger" which has intruded into our tradition. Haughty sentiments, however momentary, are an obstacle to *ahimsa because they cause harm*; and keeping for oneself what the world needs is another "obstacle"—a kind of violence, and a source of further violence. Here are pride and covetousness, and the ideals of humility and poverty, in a new perspective. Fear and haste are "enemies" in the Hindu tradition of non-violence which are not commonly thought of as "vices" in Christianity; and yet they are, as a moment's reflection will show, very common sources of violent behaviour. We are not accustomed to thinking of them as "enemies" or "vices". Yet our own tradition teaches us in the strongest terms that love casts out *fear*, and the lilies of the field should be for us a lasting warning against fear in its most commonplace form, which is worry. As for haste, the mustard-seed and the leaves have something to do with that; and it was precisely because Jesus refused to be in a "violent hurry" to establish his kingdom, in the way some of the Jews demanded, that the violence implicit in their demand turned against him, and pinned him to the Cross.

Christians could do no more appropriate service to the Church and the world at the present time than to explore the traditions of non-violence, and restore them to a central place in Christian lives; provided, that is, that they always remember two things. First, that non-violence is for the spiritually strong, rather than for the weak. It is nothing else but spiritual force in the service of love; the discipline of non-violence is concerned with a transformation of spiritual energy, and makes no sense if there is no energy to transform. The gentleness of the weak is of no more significance than the chastity of the impotent. Secondly, the purpose of educating violence out of the personality, for the Christian, is to educate compassion into it; especially that supreme compassion, which is love of enemies.

Beyond the foothills are the mountains that are not so easily conquered. Behind the commonplace fear looms the primitive dread, behind the ordinary anger the primitive hate, beyond the ordinary haste the will to power; and just as, to a mountaineer, a mountain is both friend and enemy, so the primitive passions we have to conquer, whether in ourselves or others, provide the means of our ascent. For Christians to follow this way is to follow the steps of their master.

To shatter the primitive pattern of violent response is to shatter a pattern which makes sense in terms of self-preservation. Ultimately, this can only be done by virtue of a vision which makes better sense, and which has its origin beyond the natural world. The higher ascents of non-violence are only for those who are roped by faith.

2. THE NECESSARY ACCOMMODATION: THE CLAIMS OF THE WORLD

It might be objected that all this is very remote from the problem of international relations, and the challenge of the Bomb; it may be all right as an ideal of personal behaviour, but it does not resolve any political issue.

In a sense, this is true; the early Christians thought that the way to resolve political problems was simply to extend the charity of their personal behaviour into the public sphere, and this is too easy a view—the public act has its own special complexity.

On the other hand, it is clear that there is a certain continuity between the individual's moral attitudes and the behaviour of his group. Two things can happen in the group to concentrate and multiply the violence of individuals within the group. One is projection—the arrogance, haughtiness, disdain and greed which are partially suppressed in the individual can be projected in alarming proportions and enjoyed in the behaviour of the group, where they win social approval by disguising themselves as "loyalty", and so cease to be restrained, as they are on the personal level, by social pressures. Another process is the snowballing of hatreds which occurs when small resentments combine to seek out a common enemy or scapegoat. On a small scale the thing can be observed in any neighbourhood gossip group, when a few people find they share a scarcely definable antagonism to some other individual. Give them a few minutes to roll together their antagonisms, and a much more potent compound will emerge—the unfortunate victim will be hard put to it to re-establish his shattered reputation. Even those who did not share in the original antagonism may be drawn into the attack in order to "belong" to the group.

On a national scale, it is usually under stress of war

that this process is most in evidence, but the dangers are always present. We may think, for instance, with justifiable horror, of the mass-extermination of Jews in Hitler's Germany and be convinced that *we* could never be implicated in such conduct. But what of the "slight antagonism" we feel towards such and such a person, or group—or nation? Only a slight antagonism, maybe, a far cry from murder; but once let this antagonism be shared by a large number of people, once let it breed, let it be given effective leadership, fostered by propaganda and harnessed to the impersonal techniques of modern science, and we may be nearer to murder than we thought. Every man who hates his brother, said St John, is a murderer—and in group hatreds the inner truth of this often becomes a hideous reality. Again, we may laugh at the concept of the "master race", and feel sure that we are far from such absurdity. But what of the slight scorn we feel for those of such and such a religion, or colour, or nationality? A justifiable excess of zeal, or of patriotism, one might think, hardly a blemish on a Christian character; but once let this arrogance fester among millions, let it be given a creed and a purpose, and we may soon find ourselves involved in group attitudes quite as ridiculous as that of the "master race" in the eyes of the rest of the world.

People who are aware of the seeds of violence in the human personality can help to frustrate these dangerous cumulative processes at an early stage—they will be poor recipients of propaganda, and will not readily find themselves involved in a crusade of hatred against a Makarios, a Soekarno or a Mao Tse-tung, simply because they read the *Daily Blast*. There is good reason to suppose, then, that the exploration of non-violence on a personal level is relevant, and will in the long run be profoundly relevant, to the large-scale problem of violence which confronts the human race.

At the same time, this does not solve the immediate political problems; and since the immediate problems are the most real and urgent, to avoid them may be very much like avoiding reality altogether. It is just at this point that tension between the world and the Gospels is at its greatest, and it is just here that the idealist can go astray through an inability to make the right kind of accommodation.

It is so easy to approach the problem of group or political action by asking, not, "What is possible, or appropriate, in this situation?" but rather "What would I do, if I and I alone were my country, and if I were loyal to my personal ideals? How would I have acted, if I and I alone were Kennedy and his advisers, when he had to make his decisions about Cuba?" or, "How would I hope to behave, if I alone were India, threatened with a Chinese invasion?" Unfortunately, the political meditations which emerge from such heart-searchings are likely to be just about as politically relevant as Walter de la Mare's delightful poem about the King of Tartary, and to leave the thinker in a similar childhood wonderland.

There are many reasons why it is unreal to think of the group or political act in this way. Most obviously, the national group is a collection of people of varying degrees of moral awareness, with complex material and intellectual vested interests, a curious mixture of

6*

fear, selfishness, greed, self-assertion—and generosity. They will only be led where they are prepared to go, and, although this may not be very far, it is important to lead them gently, so that they can gain confidence to go further. Significant progress is made only when convenience and morality enter into a secret conspiracy.

Even if all the members of the group were of the same moral quality, and had similar interests, it still would not follow that the appropriate group act in a particular situation could be just a projection of the individual act on to a large screen. Human words and actions take their meaning not only from the "inner" soul of a man, but also from their context, their setting, their tradition; and what we can say and mean is therefore limited in each situation; but the acceptance of this limitation is a condition of creative thought and action. The different contexts in which we act therefore impose, to some extent, a different pattern of meaning upon us; and the international political act takes place in its own special context, which is different from the personal one, and has its own constituted meanings, its own inescapable traditions, and its own peculiar possibilities and limitations. Nothing could be more urgent than to play a creative role in developing this language; but it is necessary first to learn it.

All this is likely to be very discouraging to the sensitive idealist, and to the man of high moral integrity, who sees his ideals marred by compromise; and the temptation is strong to consign politics, especially of the international kind, to the amoral outer darkness. Unfortunately, in the outer darkness lurk demons who are only too willing to take over the wheel which the idealist has left idle, and to steer his boat on to rocks which he could have avoided.

Against this, it will be argued that the Christian, who after all does not belong heart and soul to this world, must reserve to himself the ultimate right of refusal, of rejecting and of cutting himself off from a society which is irretrievably committed to evil ways, when there seems to be no possibility of morally good political action, and the only ultimate moral resource is a resounding "No!" to what is going on. Certainly this could be the case, and would probably be the case in any future national war. But many pacifists, both in Britain and in the States, would argue that this is already the case—that both nations are already irretrievably committed to threats of mass violence which are the greatest imaginable contradiction to the non-violence which is the heart of Christianity, and that there is no really possible political alternative. Accommodation to this situation is therefore a betrayal, and only the ultimate protest is valid.

It is, of course, true that unilateral disarmament is not practical politics in the States, and that getting out of NATO is not practical politics in Britain; so that any practical policy could be regarded as a kind of acceptance of massive violence, or of the "nuclear umbrella". It is possible to see this deterrent policy as nothing but a projection into the group of all that is evil and primitive in the individual; and this is partly true. But before deciding therefore to turn our backs on the historical process, it may be well to ask whether the deterrent policy, which is a group attitude in a definite historical and international context, has not some meaning in that context which we can make sense of, a meaning which we can in some way assume, in order to speak in the real language of international history, and to play a positive and creative role in this history at its moment of crisis.

If our analysis of the situation is correct, the meaning which is emerging out of the deterrent policy for the whole international community is nothing else than the ultimate futility of massive violence—that is, of international war—as a means of resolving human conflicts. It is a meaning that is gradually becoming clear, a lesson that is slowly being learnt, as the stalemate of violence spreads its influence, and multiplying problems become less and less amenable to violent resolution.

Does this not mean that the sooner all armaments are scrapped the better, and that, if the futility of violence is the point, nothing could be more sensible than unilateralism? Unfortunately, the sense which is embedded in the real situation is of a different kind. The futility of violence, which is in essence to do with the nature of violence itself, is only *evident to the world* through the balance between the great opponents. Here is violent stimulus – violent response frozen on a massive scale, a great object lesson to humanity, pointing it and forcing it towards a new pattern of international society. It can be said, therefore, that those politicians and military strategists who specialize in perfecting the balance, in making the "second-strike" capacity invulnerable, are doing something relevant, something that makes a kind of sense, even if that sense is at present a little beyond the limits of their comprehension.

But is this reading of the situation too remote from the intention of the protagonists, too remote from the meaning the world sees, to be valid? Perhaps; but there are indications that it is not so remote—that the meaning is already there, in an inchoate form, in the minds both of the protagonists themselves, and in the third world which views their actions. It is a commonplace, for instance, that "the purpose of the deterrent is *not to be used*". Advanced deterrent thinkers in the States are showing an increasing concern that the Russians should *keep up*,[9] in order that the balance should be preserved, the stalemate perpetuated, and violence remain inoperative—though they have not yet reached the logical conclusion of exporting Polaris to Russia! Both sides show an increasing and *united* concern to avoid the spread of nuclear weapons, and the suggestion of bomber bonfires, though at present it only applies to obsolete weapons, at least shows a significant direction of thought. Meanwhile, recourse to the machinery of justice to resolve disputes instead of to war, recourse to the UN, to arbitration, to conferences, to treaties, is becoming increasingly urgent, increasingly commonplace, and given a small amount of goodwill, increasingly successful. The balance has something to do with all this.

Of course, the situation is highly dangerous. The balance is never really stable, the danger of war by accident is substantial, and the prospect of the proliferation of nuclear weapons is a grim one. The danger, however, is inevitable; we are in it—whatever we do will certainly be dangerous. The sensible question is, is there a valid way forward, in the direction of history, out of the danger? If the nuclear deterrence of the major powers were nothing else than the sum total of all that is violent, evil and primitive in humanity, then certainly nothing but protest and pessimism would be justified. But even if these attitudes have their historical origins in violent and primitive reactions, it does not follow that their present meaning can be understood fully in terms of these origins. It may be that humanity can use, and is beginning to use this situation as a device for heaving itself laboriously up a great rock in the evolutionary climb. If this is so, then a qualified optimism is justified; and, since we are all on this climb whether we like it or not, some kind of intelligent co-operation may be required.

It could be put in another way. The world wars which have shaken our generation could be the death-throes of a civilization unable to respond to the challenges presented to it by its own advance; or, on the other hand, they could be the first stage of labour, the pangs which would announce the birth of a new international order. The present nuclear stalemate, and the series of crises which have characterized it, could be the death agony, or they could be the last constrictions which accompany the birth. History will judge what we cannot see. Meanwhile, there is the dreadful ambiguity; and for Christians, as always, the Gospels, the world, and a heavy but perplexing responsibility.

3. A NEW CRUSADE: THE WORLD AND THE GOSPELS

A mood of puzzlement and frustration, however, would be neither useful nor appropriate in the present world crisis. The challenge which faces humanity demands a vigorous response. What we need is a new crusade, a new sense of communal purpose, inspired by a dynamic vision of man's destiny—something like that vision which set the people of Europe on the road to Jerusalem at the end of the eleventh century. Only this time, we hope, the vision will be better grounded in reality, and the crusaders more fully equipped with a knowledge of the human condition, and with a knowledge of the Gospels.

How are we to think of this crusade?

Not, perhaps, as a crusade of *charity*; for, central as this idea is in theological discourse, there are aspects of the tradition of charity which make it an awkward tool at the present time.

Charity and justice are commonly contrasted; and Christian charity has been traditionally associated with the relief of suffering—alms for the poor, homes for the homeless, hospitals for the sick, and so on. These have traditionally been works of charity, and *not of justice*; and, partly because of this, "charity" has often failed to attack in an organized way the causes of the evils which it has sought to alleviate; for it is justice which forms the structure of society, which asserts rights and obligations, and founds the laws by which we live. The great problems which face the world today, the enmity of embattled nations and the widening gap between rich and poor, are indeed challenges to charity; but nothing would be a greater mistake than to think that they can be cured just by kindness. Both of these problems demand a radical restructuring of international society, requiring us to reappraise our own nation and others in the new light of an overriding world-loyalty, in the context of a massive and universal assertion of the rights of man. The early Christians, a "specialist" group within a stable order, were not immediately concerned with the structure of society; but today, after two thousand years, both the leaven and the loaf have changed their nature. Now, problems of structure and order are the most urgent issues facing mankind; and we must all face them together.

What of the contrary tradition, then; could we think of a crusade of justice?

This is much more to the point; but again, there are elements in the tradition of justice which cause misgivings. Justice does indeed concern itself with the structural problems of society; but it has sometimes been in danger of "freezing up"—of "fixing" a situation by putting it into a strait-jacket of abstract rights and duties, and thereby excluding the notion of radical change. The "just-war" tradition to some extent did this in regard to the question of war, and "natural-law" theorists once did it in regard to slavery. If this freezing takes place, it is likely to freeze out both the world and the Gospels; for the world is changing at a staggering rate, and the Gospels open up an unlimited perspective.

This is not to say that charity and justice are not two of the most precious concepts in our Christian tradition. Together, they are able to transform the world; like the left and right eye of the conscience, they function together to give us an adequate grasp of reality, and enable us to act effectively in the world. If justice constitutes the body politic, charity is its very life-blood; charity without justice spills out and is lost; but justice without charity constitutes not a living body, but a dry and lifeless corpse.

What is required for our new crusade is an idea which will transcend the apparent opposition, include what is vital in both justice and charity, and at the same time be fully relevant both to the world and to the Gospels.

Perhaps we should think, then, of a crusade of *fellowship*. For to think of fellowship is immediately to think of a common undertaking, a partnership within a single legal structure; to think of building fellowship is to think of the discovery of a common task within the framework of a common law. Fellowship then demands justice—the assertion of rights, the construction of institutions, the formation of laws. At the same time, fellowship points to charity; for a fellow is one for whom one has "fellow-feeling"—not the sympathy of condescension, but the sympathy of identification—a love, that is, which includes a radical assertion of equality, that very equality which is also the first demand of justice. Justice and charity come together in a new perspective, that of the universal community of men.

The idea is not unscriptural. We know that Jesus was primarily concerned with the world's outcasts, with the deprived, the despised, the sinners and the sufferers; and his typical action towards them was the act of fellowship—to eat with them. We think of him, for example, inviting himself to supper with Zacchaeus, who had climbed a tree to see him pass. When he is asked by the Pharisees, "Who is my neighbour?" he answers with the story of the Good Samaritan, in which the hero is a member of a despised and heretical sect, near neighbours of the orthodox Jews. The story has a double level of meaning. It teaches, by the actions of the Samaritan, that it is for every man to assert his kinship with those in need; and it teaches us, by the fact that he is a Samaritan, that the members of the sect or the nation we condemn as "heretics" may well be worthier in the eyes of God than ourselves, and that their worth, like ours, will be judged by their ability to take in Jesus's answer to the Pharisees' question, "Who is my neighbour?"

The ministry of healing can be understood in the same light. In laying his hands on the sick, Jesus asserted his fellowship with them, and at the same time gave them back to the community from which they had been separated by their disease; for sickness is divisive. In the same way, the forgiveness of sins was a means of restoring a community which had been broken. Finally, it was through being "lifted up" that Jesus foresaw he would "draw all men to himself"; and it is in the Crucifixion and the Resurrection that the final barriers of hatred and death are overcome. It is here that the intimate connection between non-violence and fellowship becomes apparent; for the supreme fellowship-making act is also the supreme act of non-violence. Non-violence is nothing else than a radical assertion of fellowship.

The idea is also by no means irrelevant to the problems of social justice, or to the larger problems of international conflict, with which we must be concerned. If a new international order is struggling into being, nothing could be more appropriate, or more in line with the principle of fellowship, than to help it on its way. To assist at its birth may be a unique privilege that providence is offering to this generation. There should be something here to arouse the crusading zeal in our twentieth-century hearts, and set us off on the road to Geneva and Turtle Bay with something of the spirit in which our ancestors once set off with their carts on the road to Jerusalem.

But how and where is this to be done? Where is the rallying-point for this crusade, and what is its route? One of the penalties of the higher stage of consciousness which we have reached is that we each have to work this out for ourselves. There is a vast amount to be done on the personal level, and on the commercial, cultural and scientific levels, to improve communications, and to strengthen the infrastructure of world peace. The scope for peacemaking in all these spheres is increasing rapidly, and there is ample room for fresh initiative. The large problems of international conflict, however, still dominate the scene, and it is at this level that wars take shape.

In Britain, at the time of writing, there are signs of a new political line-up, between the independent-deterrent enthusiasts and the no-independent-deterrent enthusiasts, between those who would give less and those who would give more to strengthen the structure of the UN. The cynic or the idealist might see the distinction as morally unimportant—the one might say that it was only the expense of Polaris which was causing the trouble, the other that neither party is prepared to abandon an immoral stance. Both comments would, in a sense, be right, and both, in another sense, irrelevant. For this line-up has that mixture of moral triviality and really significant direction peculiar to political groupings. It is, in an important sense, a line-up between the more and the less world-centred view, a lesser and a greater attachment to an old pattern of national sovereignty, focused on the only issue in which, at present, it can become "incarnate". The new line-up between the more and the less internationally conscious is a feature of the politics of many countries —including those of the States, and even of "one-party" Russia, where the central debate is over peaceful-co-existence. It may be that the Socialist-Anti-socialist football teams will be replaced on the world's pitch by two different teams, in a match of far greater significance for the human race.

The problem of disarmament is part of the problem of order. Any pressure for disarmament must be linked to the construction of a valid world order, the essential features of which will be increased legislative and executive power in the UN, efficient international security and inspection forces, and greater competence for the International Court of Justice—the world judicial organ which is at present kept "judicially" in the background, but which could have some interesting observations to make on a number of disputed issues if it were given a chance. Progress in disarmament will always be related to progress in order, and the long debate over inspection is just one aspect of this. The just-war thinkers had this much to be said for them; they were right in thinking international violence could be seen as an attempt to do something which had to be done—to establish international justice. It is now very obvious that it cannot perform this function; but international violence certainly will not wither away unless there is something to fill the gap. The stalemate of violence is a terrifying schoolmaster; but he will not leave us until we have learnt his lesson, and written out the exercise.

All this may seem very mundane in a "religious" light. Is it not mere international humanism, without supernatural perspective, neglecting altogether the spheres of grace and redemption? What is specifically *Christian* about it?

Certainly, the Christian may find himself facing the same problems as the "humanist", and answering them in the same kind of way; he is, after all, human. The Word of God does indeed give him a direction; but it is not a "first-right-second-left" sort of direction; it is rather the kind of direction the sun gives when it rises in the East. It is still for the Christian, in community with his fellows, to examine the lie of the land, to choose the way, to make the paths which will lead towards the light. But the Christian's vision, precisely in so far as it is Christian, is not mundane. His faith gives to his sense of communion, to his understanding of sacrifice, a deeper perspective, a different dimension. For that very reason he has the more cause to rejoice if the world moves towards greater fellowship and the rejection of violence; for this is, however remotely, the direction of Christ.

At the same time, the Christian's faith concerns the present as well as the future. The effective kingship of the risen Christ, and his relationship to every human being, makes a startling difference here and now to our picture of the human race, and of every individual human being; and the communion liturgy through which, despite our efforts to disguise it, he has established in the ordinary world a new and prophetic fellowship, gives us an infinite perspective into the present, as well as into the future.

The Christian, above all, will be fired by a sense of man's hidden but infinite potentiality for fellowship and for joy, with a hope that is too firmly grounded to be extinguished by pain, disappointment, or death. For him the words of Isaiah will be at once a great hope, a great reality, and an inspiration to action:

> And they shall repair the waste cities, the desolations
>   of many generations,
> Violence shall be no more heard in thy land,
> Wasting nor destruction within thy borders;
> But thou shalt call thy walls salvation,
> And thy gates praise.[10]

NOTES

[1] Jas. 3.10.
[2] 1 John 3.15.
[3] 1 Pet. 4.18.
[4] Quoted by Régamey, O.P., *Non-violence et conscience hrétienne*, Paris (1958), p. 212.

[5] Luke 9.54–5.
[6] Especially Régamey, *Non-violence*.
[7] Matt. 5.45.
[8] Régamey, pp. 211ff.
[9] e.g. Morgenstern, in *Questions of National Defense*, Random House (1959); quoted by Strachey, p. 828.
[10] Isa. 40.18.

INDEX